CW01670189

Bristol: maritime city

Frank Chipsides —

Robert Wall

BRISTOL: maritime city

Frank Shipsides and Robert Wall

THE REDCLIFFE PRESS
BRISTOL

First published in November 1981 by
Redcliffe Press Ltd, Bristol

© Frank Shipsides and Robert Wall

To the seamen of
Bristol, past,
present, and yet to
come

All rights reserved. No part of this publication may be reproduced, stored in a retrieval system, or transmitted, in any form or by any means, electronic, mechanical, photocopying, recording or otherwise, without the prior permission of the publishers.

ISBN 0 905459 37 7

Printed in Great Britain by
Burleigh Ltd, Bristol

Contents

Acknowledgements

The authors are grateful to the many people who helped in the preparation of this book, and in particular the following members of the Port of Bristol Authority: Stanley Turner, General Manager; Captain Tony Gibbons and Commander Joe Bradley, Havenmasters; John Corin, Rodney Stone, Michael Griffiths and Richard Jones of the Port's Public Relations Department.

From the City of Bristol: Dudley Lewis, Deputy City Clerk of Bristol; Douglas Harmer, Administrator of the City Museum and Art Gallery; Arnold Wilson, Director of the City Art Gallery; Paul Elkin, Technical Curator, City Museum and from Avon County Council, the Staff of Westbury-on-Trym Library. From Bristol's shipping industry in its many forms: Hubert Ashmead, Peter Ashmead, Commander Joe Blake, Basil Brown, Noel Brown, Jim Crissup, George Deverson, Ernest Dumbleton, Tim Healy, John Hill, Richard Hill, Alan Stevenson, Alderman L. K. Stevenson, Roger Stevenson, Pilot Bert Watkins.

Miss Alyson Reeves and Mrs. Susan Rzeznicki helped with the preparation of the manuscript and the advice of our publisher John Sansom was of great help and comfort, as was that of the partners of Alexander Gallery, John Cleverdon and Jim Fardon.

We are grateful to Macmillan & Co for permission to quote from Rudyard Kipling—*The Coastwise Lights*; to Gollancz for Dorothy L. Sayers—*The English War*; to Gerald Duckworth for Hilaire Belloc—*The South Country* and to Sir John Betjeman and John Murray for *Bristol*.

Finally, we thank our wives Phyl Shipsides and Jean Wall who have had to endure the domestic upheaval that writing and illustrating a book inevitably produces. Without their support and understanding this book would not have appeared.

Preface

THERE ARE several reasons why the present time is appropriate for the appearance of a general history of the Port of Bristol. First, there is the preoccupation of Bristol and its citizens with port affairs which has persisted in recent years and the problems of port finance and development which have still to be resolved. A reminder of how past generations faced similar tasks may be useful. Second, although there are many specialist books and monographs on the port, and several excellent city histories have been published recently, it is seventy-two years since Charles Wells published his *A Short History of the Port of Bristol* and much has happened in Bristol's maritime history since then.

Above all, there is the opportunity to continue the study of Bristol through the eyes and skill of Frank Shipsides, who extends in this volume the remarkable collection of paintings and drawings previously published by The Redcliffe Press in *Bristol Impressions* and *Bristol: Profile of a City*. Once again he has captured that special ambience of Bristol that makes our city so popular with visitors and so loved by residents. In addition, this latest assembly of marine paintings and drawings makes, I believe, a major contribution to Bristol maritime art, so vividly demonstrated in the early years of this century by Wilde Parsons, and by a long line of local painters back to the time of Nicholas Pocock.

Finally, this book is not intended to be a formal history but rather a celebration of the 'City and County and Port of Bristol', as the old toastmasters put it, and of its citizens, merchants and seamen all. Long may they prosper!

Bristol, November 1981 Robert Wall

*'The men who live in West England, they see the Severn strong,
Rolling on dark waters brown, light aspen leaves along,
They have the secret of the rocks and the oldest kind of song.'*

Hilaire Belloc—*The South Country.*

Picking up the Bristol Pilot at the Breaksea.

The Bristol Channel

THE SEVERN, most English of all rivers, rises on Plynlimmon, a Welsh fastness, two and a half thousand feet up in the air and two hundred miles from the sea. The longest river in Britain, it hastens out of Wales to wander gently and almost aimlessly through the broad farmlands of Shropshire, Worcestershire and Gloucestershire. This is the river of Elgar, who crossed it daily on his journeys into Worcester, his head full of tunes of glory. From the Malvern Hills beyond, Langland saw the Severn in the vale on a May morning, and dreamed of Piers Plowman. Further south, the young Charles II climbed his royal oak to hide from Cromwell's Ironsides. Shakespeare's Avon joins at Tewkesbury, scene of the last fight of Simon de Monfort, sire of the Mother of Parliaments.

South of Gloucester, the Severn meets the muddy saltwater of the Bristol Channel for the first time. At certain high tides in the year, the Channel tide rolls back the advancing Severn water to create a spectacular bore, a tidal wave that can reach a height of six feet or more, sweeping silently up river. Then, in the space of a few miles, the banks of the river diverge. The northern shore swings round the Forest of Dean to meet the Wye and pass west to Wales, while the southside leaves Berkeley, with its memories of the petulant Edward II and the life-saving genius of Edward

Jenner, and breasts the cliffs of Aust to run down to Avonmouth.

From shore to shore hereabouts, the Severn Road Bridge spans the river, with 3,240 feet of decking between its main piers. Opened by Queen Elizabeth II in 1966, it is among the world's top dozen suspension bridges, and guards the northern limits of the Bristol Channel.

To gaze southwestwards from the Severn Bridge on an evening in early summer is to look on an estuary which outwardly is at peace. The setting sun angles its light from behind the hills of Gwent to strike the mudbanks and flats of the river and turn them to the texture of burnished steel.

The illusion is momentary, however. For this Channel is among the most active waters on the planet. Twice in every natural day, the tidal flow of the Bristol Channel gathers its strength in the waters around Lundy, and charges bull-headed north-easterly upstream. In doing so, it produces spring tides at Avonmouth, for example, of forty-two feet, and the restless waters carry vast quantities of sediment. Approximately two million tons of mud are carried past Severn Beach on an ebb tide. By the time the gathering waves reach Avonmouth and meet the constricting banks of the Severn for the first time, the tidal range has become high indeed. At Beachley it has been known to reach fifty feet. That is, fifty feet of vertical rise from low water to high. As any Bristol schoolchild will tell you, in only one other part of the world is there a higher tidal range. This is in the Bay of Fundy, on the east coast of Canada between Nova Scotia and New Brunswick, where the tide produces a similar bore on the Petitcodiac river.

To the stranger who does not know the Channel, this tidal range is staggering. In the course of a tide, the raging torrent of the river is transformed into idle mudflats and pleasant looking sandbanks which the ignorant would imagine to be excellent places for a gallop.

As the tide flows back to the sea so the tributary rivers empty, and what fresh water still runs is a minute stream at the bottom of thirty feet high mudbanks. It is a common practice of Bristolians to take visiting naval officers to look at the Avon at low tide, and then let them imagine what would happen to their ship if ever they were trapped by the falling waters!

South-west from Bristol and Avonmouth, the Bristol Channel flows on

The training ship, Formidable, *moored in Kingroad from 1869 to 1906, is passed by the pilot cutter* Marguerite.

FRANK SHIPSIDES 1981

FRANK SHIPSIDES 198

to the sea. Here it meets the first of the islands, a small pimple of rock on the Denny Shoal, and as the waters broaden, soon the contrasting isles of Flatholm and Steepholm appear, set in the water to form a series of giant stepping stones with Brean Down and Crook Peak on the southern shore. The islands look like something left over by the Creator when He built the Mendip Hills. From these islands, the Channel rolls home to the sea, 40 miles on to the grim granite of Lundy which stands abreast the Atlantic Ocean and where the sea properly begins.

Almost as soon as he began to think and became conscious that wood floats on water, man attempted to sail the waters of this vast estuary. There are hut circles on Lundy that some scholars ascribe to the Neolithic period, about 3,500 years BC. If they are correct then these men could have only come from the mainland as Lundy became separated from the Devon coast at the end of the last Ice Age. There is plenty of evidence on the islands of the Channel to show that Bronze Age Man and his Iron Age successors travelled frequently between the islands and the coast. Soon the Roman legions appeared, 'striding out to Severn', as Chesterton wrote, under the command of Ostorius Scapula, although legend has it that they first crossed the river by the sandbanks at Newnham, chest high in water. It is also alleged that they once lost a full legion during a night crossing. Later, St. Augustine also came this way.

The Romans were excellent seamen and they established a channel tradition. From the Roman Age on, the Channel became a broad highway to the sea and men from both banks used it to start those journeys to lands of which even 'Caesar never dreamed'.

Although they did not realise it, the Romans lit on one of the geographical reasons for the later foundation of the City of Bristol. From Land's End north-eastwards along the rough coasts of Cornwall and Devon, and the mudflats of the Somerset estuaries, there is no real harbour where a fleet of any size can take refuge. But in the Avon, flowing down to the Severn, the Romans discovered safe anchorage for their ships. At Sea Mills they built a small harbour from which stores could be ferried across to the great legion depot at Isca.

As Roman power waned, and the Angles, Saxons, Danes and finally

Evening in the City Docks.

A map of the Bristol Channel.

the Normans invaded England from the east in succession, the Bristol Channel area lay on the westward fringes of history and probably took little part in the main stream of events. Yet sometime after the last Roman had departed and before the Norman cavalry chased Harold's beaten Saxons from Senlac Hill, someone in the west took council with a group of his neighbours and founded a town which he called 'the place of the bridge'. The bridge spanned the Avon near present day Welsh Back, and the town was to become the City of Bristol, and England's natural gateway to the western world.

When a city is built at the junction of two rivers and only five miles from the largest estuary in the land, it is inevitable that maritime affairs become woven into the destiny of its citizens. In the two millenia that have followed, the ships of Bristol have carried the name of the City and, more importantly, its cargoes to the world. Sometimes, the ships have not returned. Often they have returned empty or damaged, with tales to tell of sea fights and death, but more often than not, they have returned with riches on which the wealth and prosperity of generations has been based.

Today, in the twentieth century, the world's ships come to Bristol. Let us, in the mind's eye, join one such visitor coming up Channel, passing the South Light of Lundy on an evening tide in summer.

On the port side, the island lies tranquil, the church built by the aptly named Reverend Heaven and the Old Light standing stark against the sky. The Society of Merchant Venturers of Bristol, who will take some prominence in these pages, provided the first Channel lights, because they were the Bristol Channel Light Authority for over two centuries. The Old Light on Lundy was built by Trinity House in 1819, but in bad weather the lantern, over 560 feet above the sea, was often hidden in cloud, so new lights at the north and south ends of the island were built in 1897. Northward the hills of the Gower appear on the horizon, while to the south, the nearest land is marked by the great white tower of the lighthouse on Hartland Point. Hereabouts, and eastwards beyond Porlock and Minehead, the coast consists of steep cliffs where man has only penetrated to the sea down wooded valleys at such places as Clovelly, Ilfracombe and Lynmouth. Hartland was the 'Hercules Point' of old:

> 'Where, on Hartland's tempest furrowed shore,
> Breaks the long swell from fartherest Labrador . . .'

Past Lundy, the Bristol Channel begins. East of the island, in Lundy Roads, there is a good anchorage, protected from the prevailing south westerlies. Here it was that the Bristol pilots of old cruised in their skiffs, seeking ships needing pilotage to Bristol. Even today, Bristol pilots occasionally board the largest inbound ships in these waters, using boats from Ilfracombe.

From Hartland Point, it is forty-seven miles north-north-westward across Lundy to St. Ann's Head Lighthouse at the entrance to Milford Haven, the northern bastion of the Bristol Channel. As we cross this line we enter the Channel and set course for the Breaksea Light where our pilot from Bristol awaits us. We run eastwards helped by a tidal stream of two knots, which the rapidly narrowing estuary will force up to three knots at the Breaksea, and even to four off Weston-super-Mare as the time for high water approaches.

Lundy falls astern, and we recall the uncomfortable official language of the *Admiralty Pilot* (the navigator's handboook): 'The island affords shelter for vessels struggling westward: no other refuge of much value offering nearer than Cardiff or Penarth Roads, 60 miles to leeward'!

Our route up to Breaksea crosses the northern edges of Barnstaple Bay, with its memories of Clovelly, the fishing village nailed to the cliffside where the occasional donkey still takes supplies down the cobbled street (the cars cheat by taking a hidden private road to the shoreline!). Then, on past Ilfracombe with its twin hills of Hillsborough and Capstone, and soon the Foreland, 720 feet high, and the most prominent point for miles, comes in sight two miles north-east of Lynmouth. Here another of the Channel lighthouses shines out as the evening darkens and we steer away north-eastward to cross the compulsory pilotage line near the Breaksea Light beacon.

Across the estuary, on the cliffs of the Welsh coast, the black and white bands of Nash Point Lighthouse have disappeared in the evening glow, but its light blinks out, singling it out from the stump of the old lighthouse nearby.

The Breaksea Light vessel, anchored half way between Bristol and Lundy, for years marked the 'Piccadilly Circus' of the Bristol Channel. Here, at the entrance to Barry Roads, ships bound for or clearing the big ports, Cardiff, Newport, Avonmouth and Bristol, all took on or dropped the pilot. Often ten or a dozen vessels would be underway, while others would anchor to await the tide, or to be signalled that a berth awaited them.

The lightship presided over these arrivals and departures, its comforting red hull ever-present in fog, sunshine, gale or breeze. Then, on April 16th 1978, it was towed away, to be replaced by an unmanned automatic beacon, as the Elder Brethren of Trinity House sought more economic methods of discharging their responsibilities. A similar fate had earlier befallen the English and Welsh Grounds Light vessel which warned of the great sandbank that divides the deep water channels leading to Newport and Bristol. It was replaced in February 1976.

A dark-hulled launch now approaches us at speed. Flying the international code flag H, this will be one of the pilot cutters of the Bristol Pilotage Authority and, likely as not, will be the *George Ray*, named after the Pill seaman who piloted the Cabots out of Bristol in 1497.

The pilot joins us on the bridge, after his leap from the pilot boat to a distinctly frail looking rope ladder which trails down the ship's side. This is an easy manoeuvre in fair weather, but in stormy seas every pilot literally takes his life in his hands, as ships are boarded at all hours, day and night, winter and summer. Yet the man who has joined us and who is quietly giving the helmsman a new bearing to steer, looks, in his sober lounge suit, more used to a city office than the bridge of a merchantman. Yet, he has the unmistakable air of one who exercises authority, and it comes as no surprise to learn that he is a qualified master mariner of proven experience.

Our journey up-channel resumes. The lights of Weston-super-Mare appear on the starboard bow, blotted out one after the other by the dark mass of Steepholm, the island now maintained as a nature reserve in memory of the late Kenneth Alsop, author and commentator. To port, the lighthouse on Flatholm, the twin island, flashes out its red and white signal, a mariner's guide since it was built in 1737. Tonight the island's foghorn, said to be the loudest in the Channel, is silent.

The Holms have acquired a goodly list of legends in the centuries that men have used them as guard houses or for refuge. Githa, mother of King Harold, lived on Steepholm after the Conquest, and is said to have died there. One can believe in the island as a place of safety. Its cliffs soar 400

Sea Mills Dock today is a quiet creek where the River Trym joins the Avon. At this point, the Roman port of Abona was founded in the first century A.D. Later, in 1712, Franklin built the third wet dock in England here, and the remains can still be seen.

feet straight out of the sea, and there is only one landing place. Today, the Victorian gun emplacement and World War II barracks are deserted, and the sea birds reign supreme.

With the Holms astern, and Clevedon to starboard, the lights of Portishead power station slowly appear, marking the four great chimneys that in daylight serve as a beacon for seamen and airmen alike. We slide past buoys with names like 'East Middle Ground', 'Welsh Hook', 'Avon', 'Newcombe' and then those marking the Firefly and Cockburn rocks. To starboard the ninety feet high quayside lights of Royal Portbury Dock reflect the stark gigantic silhouettes of the new container cranes, and we see now the lights of tugs, waiting to ease us through the Royal Edward Dock into our berth in Avonmouth.

We have arrived in the Port of Bristol, just one more statistic in a history that has extended over 2,000 years, and with centuries of maritime endeavour still awaiting it. The story of the port at Bristol and of its people, merchants and seamen all, will be told in the pages that follow. It is a tale of toil and frustration, venture and triumph, bloodshed and strife, poverty and wealth. Above all it is the record of the Bristolian seaman, tough, taciturn and waggish by turn, suspicious of the stranger but trusty also of the proven friend, and who always sailed his ship just that extra mile further than any other in the search for wealth and adventure.

'No city in England (London alone excepted) hath in so short a time, bred more brave and bold seamen, advantaged for western voyages by its situation.'

Thomas Fuller—*History of the Worthies of England 1662.*

Cabot's Matthew *at sea.*

Voyages of Discovery

BRISTOL IS unique among the great and ancient English cities in that there is little or no accurate record of its foundation. The first evidence of the city's existence is found on coins minted here during the reign of Ethelred the Unrede (978–1016). The earliest known example is in the Royal collection of the Kings of Sweden in Stockholm and was minted by Aelfwerd at Bricgstowe. Evidence abounds of early British settlements around the site that was later to become Bristol (the Observatory on Clifton Down stands in the centre of one) and these camps, as they are called, are dotted all across the West Country. Some of them, such as Cadbury Camp, are extensive fortifications and gave the Roman generals a severe test of their capability as they proceeded with the occupation of the island in the first century A.D.

The Romans left plentiful evidence of their residence in the Bristol region. The Severn and the country beyond was the frontier of Roman Britain and the garrisons that held back the Silures in the Welsh hills were supplied by the road that ran from their headquarters in Londinium to the great baths at Aquae Sulis, and then on to the little wharf at Abona where waited the first sophisticated ships to float on the Avon. Abona is today Sea Mills, where the remains of a Roman villa lie alongside the Portway.

Here Bristol's maritime history begins, although we know little of the age or its ships. We can suppose that the Romans used similar designs to those they perfected in the Mediterranean, and that these would have been exclusively for merchant and transport use. No longer than eighty feet or so, with a single deck, a large mainsail and oared steering—such a ship would prove quite seaworthy and in some ways similar to the trows of later centuries. There was no naval threat to the Roman command of the region and therefore no need to construct the great biremes which served so well in warmer seas. Indeed, it is unlikely that such unwieldly vessels would have survived long in the tidal flows of the river, which the Romans knew as Sabrina.

The last Roman troops withdrew from Britain in A.D. 407 and a grey fog of ignorance lies across West Country history from then until the years immediately prior to the Norman Conquest. The *Anglo-Saxon Chronicle* tells us that Bath, Gloucester and even Cirencester still retained in 577 the importance they enjoyed in Roman times, but there is no mention of Bristol. The town first occurs in the *Chronicle* in 1051 when it records that two sons of Earl Godwin sailed from the city for Ireland, when Godwin and his family were banished by Edward the Confessor. This mention of the Irish connection gives us strong reason to postulate one of the causes of Bristol's foundation.

Ireland at this time had been settled by Viking immigrants in the area of present-day Wicklow, Wexford and Waterford. Here was ready refuge for English subjects with reason to flee from the Saxon restoration of 1042. Also, and more important, trade with England grew up and Bristol would have been a natural place for ships from Ireland to call. At last, the Bristol region was no longer isolated from the west, and therefore, sometime probably around the reign of Alfred the Great (871–891) a town began to grow around the banks of the Avon, on a peninsula between it and the Frome, where ships could safely lie on the mud to be unloaded. The town was sufficiently high above the waters for its sewage to drain directly into the river. The bridge, from which the town took its name, was probably a wooden one (traces of wooden piers were found when the present Bristol Bridge was built in 1768) and the merchants built their houses on the eastern bank in the pleasant meadows of Redcliffe. If one wonders why the town was built so far from the sea, along six miles of difficult river, the answer lies in the ease with which the site could be fortified and the fact

Redcliffe Bridge in the 1950s, looking upstream to the site of Bristol's earliest port at 'the place of the bridge'. The Frome entered the Avon hereabouts before 1247.

that contemporary technology was insufficiently advanced to allow a bridge of greater size farther downstream.

The same Harold Godwinsen that fled Bristol in 1051 was crowned King of England the day after the death of the Confessor in January 1066. This was in direct contravention of his oath to support the claim of Duke William of Normandy (admittedly extracted from him by force) and led to the Norman conquest of England. In 1068, three sons of the dead Harold tried to force the passage of the Avon and sack Bristol with a fleet from Ireland but were stood off by the citizens. Indeed, Bristolians had offered no resistance to William and probably welcomed his firm rule in which they could return to their one preoccupation—trade. Nevertheless, the King ordered the construction of a large castle on the eastern wall of the town and the work was begun under the direction of Geoffrey Mowbray, Bishop of Coutances and Exeter.

The early layout of the city grew around the crossroads of four streets that still exist—Wine Street, Broad Street, Corn Street and High Street—and the bridge where High Street ended in the later St. Nicholas Gate were, together with the castle, to set the pattern of the city for the next six centuries. Here above the bridge, the ships came and went. In this era, we can deduce the size and appearance of ships from the seals of port towns that survive in civic archives. The hulls had been developed from the classic Norse longships to give larger topsides and hence better seakeeping qualities. Some of the bigger ships might have been decked in, but this only became general in the early fourteenth century. By the thirteenth century, the vessels were mostly carrying fore and sterncastles, structures above the bow and stern, which could carry archers for defence. The single mast remained with its large square rigged sail, and steering was by a single oar as in Viking times.

The earliest records carry little if any mention of Bristol's trade pattern from the tenth to twelfth centuries, but the Charters of Henry II (1155) and John (1188 approx.) provide some clues. Wool, wine, hides and corn were protected trades only to be dealt in by Bristol burgesses within the confines of the port, and there is mention of cheese and iron. Bristol provided six vessels to supply Henry's expedition to Ireland in 1171.

All around the city in these medieval times, the baronial wars that plagued England continued. Bristol was involved in the rebellion against William Rufus, then held for the King in Henry I's time by Robert Fitzhamon and Robert, Earl of Gloucester. In the dreadful civil wars of the reign of Stephen (1135–1154), Bristol was for the pretender Queen Maud, and the garrison terrorised the surrounding countryside. The consequent disorder allowed the Bristol merchants to indulge themselves in what to the popular mind has become their staple trade—slaving. This had thrived in Bristol in the days of the Conqueror and had been condemned roundly by Wulfstan, Bishop of Worcester (1062–1095). The trade was mainly with Ireland and the Bristolians were not above kidnapping any unfortunates that they could lay their hands on. Wulfstan sought the help of William himself and the trade was temporarily (and reluctantly) abandoned, but the lawlessness in the days of Stephen allowed it to restart. At last, in 1154, Stephen died. When she had first made Bristol her base, Maud had brought with her Henry, her son, then aged nine. As Stephen's heir had died the year before, the boy, still only twenty-one, took the throne as Henry II, whom later historians would identify with Elizabeth I as one of the two greatest rulers that England was to have. As mentioned above, Henry's first act was to grant Bristol a valuable charter in 1155. With the exceptions of Edward II and the Stuarts, Bristol has since maintained a watchful loyalty to the ruling family down to this day.

Bristol's trade prospered under Henry II and he even granted Dublin to the men of Bristol, although there is no evidence that they were very interested in the link.

A Roman merchantman of the third century A.D. This type of ship was the first large vessel to sail on the Avon and Severn.

By the mid-thirteenth century, trade in and out of Bristol had grown to such a degree that the mud wharves around Bristol Bridge had become inadequate to handle all the ships wishing to berth there. Quays had been built below the bridge and around the mouth of the Frome which in those days flowed into the Avon nearly half a mile upstream from where it does today. The Mayor (an office granted in 1216 by the nine year old Henry III after his coronation at Gloucester) and the burgesses faced a problem that has met various generations of their successors—what to do about the Port of Bristol?

Like all proposals that require work on the River Avon, the scheme carried out between 1240 and 1247 was a major piece of civil engineering and quite equivalent in contemporary terms to the Royal Portbury scheme of the twentieth century. It involved no less than the diversion of the Frome in a straight cut from Frome Bridge at the bottom of Broad Street (opposite St. John-on-the-Wall), through the marsh below St. Augustine's Abbey to reach the Avon. New quays were built alongside St. Stephen's Church and this fine new reach of the Frome became the main port area of the city. To dig the 'trench', the citizens had first to buy the land from the abbey authorities (hence Canons Marsh) and the new stream became the boundary between the civic and ecclesiastical domains. The work cost Bristol the huge sum of £5,000. No wonder the merchants of Redcliffe were reluctant to help until ordered to do so by the King 'for the common profit of the whole town of Bristol, as well as of your suburb . . .'. In all, the trench was 2,400 feet long, 120 feet wide and eighteen feet deep. It was a triumph for the men of Bristol who now proceeded to rebuild the bridge that crossed the Avon at the site of the old port. The quay above the bridge was abandoned and the bed of the river dried out by diverting the stream along a channel dug from near the Temple Church to Redcliff Back. This allowed the workmen to build large stone piers on the river bed which they did between 1247–9, two dams across the Avon holding back the diverted river and the tide. Wooden houses and shops were built on each side of the bridge in the fashion of London and there was a small Lady Chapel at the midpoint. It was to endure until rebuilding in 1762–8.

Following the building of the stone bridge, a work considered in the city to be second only to that of the trench and the new quays, the pattern of the

An English ship of the early fourteenth century of the type likely to have been sent from Bristol to the fleet of Edward III.

layout of the port was settled until the building of the Floating Harbour at the beginning of the nineteenth century, five and a half centuries later. From now on the city could only expand and it did so through the trade of its port. Wine was already established as a principal import. The throne enjoyed 3d. a ton duty on all wine landed by foreigners and in 1276 the tonnage was 2,055, rising to 2,787 in ten years. War with France was recurrent in those days and hit trade hard, but by 1307 it was back to 3,000 tons annually. As now, Bristol appears to have been principally an importing port, although she exported cloth, iron, lead and salted fish. It was not until the outbreak of the Hundred Years War that the wool trade began to expand under the direct encouragement of Edward III. He made Bristol one of eleven 'staple' towns to supervise the export of cloth, and the prosperity of the city developed accordingly. This was in direct contrast to the running battle that Bristolians had waged with the previous ruler, Edward II, whose capricious tax policy enraged the citizens, who rebelled twice, first in 1313 and again in 1326. This last uprising saw Edward II brought as a prisoner to Bristol and from there sent on to Berkeley Castle with a crown of twisted hay on his head and the insults of the exulting townsfolk sounding in his ears. On the night of September 21st, 1327, he was brutally killed in a regicide deliberately designed to demonstrate his flaunted homosexuality. Not a mark was found on the dead body.

In 1348, the ships of Bristol that crossed from France brought a very different kind of cargo—the Black Death, which was raging through Europe. The unhealthy sanitation of the town did not help (much of the sewage ran in open drains through the streets to the river) and a great number of people died. But this was only a short-term set-back. As the plague passed, so the trade of the city grew, so that by the middle of the century Bristol was the second town in the realm after London. In 1373, Edward III recognised its importance in his famous charter of that year. The city was dignified with the status of a county, its boundaries extended to include Clifton, Kingsdown and the entire course of the Avon to the sea, and then a reach of the Bristol Channel as far as Steepholm. Edward III had good cause to be grateful to Bristol. In 1346 the town had supplied twenty-four ships and 608 men for the French wars and in 1372 a further eleven ships were supplied to make good losses suffered in a battle off La Rochelle. Under the 1373 charter, the Mayor became a royal officer and a 'Common Council of the better and more honest men of the town' was to be elected as necessary. This set the pattern of local government for 400 years.

So Bristol, with its quay crowded with ships from France, particularly Gascons, Spain, Portugal, Ireland, Wales and occasionally Prussia, and its busy port officials collecting their dues of Murage and Quayage, passed into the fifteenth century. The port was controlled by the Mayor and Common Council (as it still is) and their authority was exercised by the water-baliff who was responsible for administration of the day-to-day

Looking down Welsh Back in the early 1900s.

FRANK SHIPSIDES 1981

BOSTON CITY
FRANK SHIPSIDES 1981

affairs. In some years, The Back (as the Avon below Bristol Bridge was called) did almost as good business as The Quay, and the two areas between them became the nation's largest port after the capital.

Bristol escaped the worst effects of the Wars of the Roses by pacifying each side in turn. Queen Margaret, wife of Henry VI was here in 1456, and was welcomed by the Mayor, William Canynges, undertaking the office for the third time. Later, in 1461, during the mayorality of Mede, Canynges, said to be a Lancastrian, was forced to entertain Edward IV, head of the Yorkist cause. William of Wyrcestre, the local historian writing in 1478, says that it cost Canynges 3,000 crowns to buy Edward off but later historians like Hunt (1878) argue that the Bristol merchant had been a Yorkist all along. The evidence is inconclusive either way.

William Canynges (born c. 1399) was the grandson of a merchant of the same name who commenced the rebuilding of St. Mary Redcliffe Church in the preceding century. The younger Canynges shared his grandfather's pre-occupation with the great church and spent much of his trading profit on its beautification. Canynges is an example of the merchants whose wealth and power were now the major force in Bristol. At the time of Edward's 1461 visit, he is reported by William of Wyrcestre to have possessed nine ships, 'in the Whole, 2,853 tons of Shipping, manned by 800 mariners'. It is likely that this was a large fleet for the times (in Richard II's reign the fleet of the whole city was put at thirty-seven) but it was not unique and shows the wealth that could be accumulated. The richer merchants lived very well and their houses around Redcliffe all possessed large cellars for merchandise, on the ground floor a warehouse and shops, and living quarters above. Behind there would be a large banqueting hall.

Like all other professions, the merchants had their trade guild. At the time of Canynges, it was the Fraternity of the Merchants and Mariners of Bristol, dedicated to God, Our Lady, St. Clement and St. George, and in 1467, when he was Mayor for the fifth and final time, he and the council delegated some of their powers of port administration to the Fraternity. In this year, the records of the Society of Merchant Venturers, heirs of the Fraternity, begin.

The City Docks in their heyday; the Bristol City Line's Boston City *discharging cargo from New York between the wars.*

So the stage was set for the 'Age of Discovery', as the latter years of the fifteenth century were called by future historians. The careful, thoughtful Henry VII, who founded the Tudor dynasty by his victory at Bosworth in 1485, was determined on peace and set out to acquire the wealth that would prevent any further upstart rebellions. The revival of interest in the arts and sciences that created the great European Renaissance inspired men to look beyond their own shores. Old ideas in science and religion were challenged and there came the dawn of an idea that the lands of the fabulous east with their trade in spices could in truth be reached by sailing west. Bristol was well placed for a such a venture and had traded in dried cod with the Icelanders for a number of years. Here, the sailors from the Avon would have heard of fabled Vinland which the Norse sagas said lay to the south west. Further voyaging was difficult, as the Danes carefully controlled trade.

Several Bristol expeditions preceded that of the Cabots in 1497. In 1480, Thomas Lloyd sailed west in an eighty ton ship owned by John Jay junior and searched for the 'Ile of Brazil'. He left Kingroad on July 15th, and spent nine weeks cruising fruitlessly in the Atlantic until at last returning to Ireland. Other voyages are said to have taken place, particularly one in 1481 by two ships, the *George* and the *Trinity*. Another unproved story is the visit to Bristol in 1477 of the young Christopher Columbus, eager to take passage westward on a Bristol ship. The possibility is that some of these voyages were in fact only out to the Porcupine Bank, a well known fishing ground to the west of Ireland.

To a Genoese, domiciled in Bristol, went the honour of eventual success, and the reward of immortality. John Cabot came to Bristol by way of Venice and settled here sometime in the 1490s. He seems to have avoided the usual Bristol suspicion of strangers, for he was a leading citizen by the end of his first years, securing letters patent from the King on March 5th, 1496 to, *inter alia,* 'sail to all parts, countries and seas of the east, of the west, and of the north . . . with five ships of what burden or quality soever they be . . . and find whatsoever isles, countries, regions or provinces of the heathens and infidels whatsoever they be . . .'.

History casts only a flickering light over the activities of John Cabot and his sons Lewis, Sebastian and Sanctius. Although there is limited evidence that Bristol ships sighted the New World years before Columbus while on

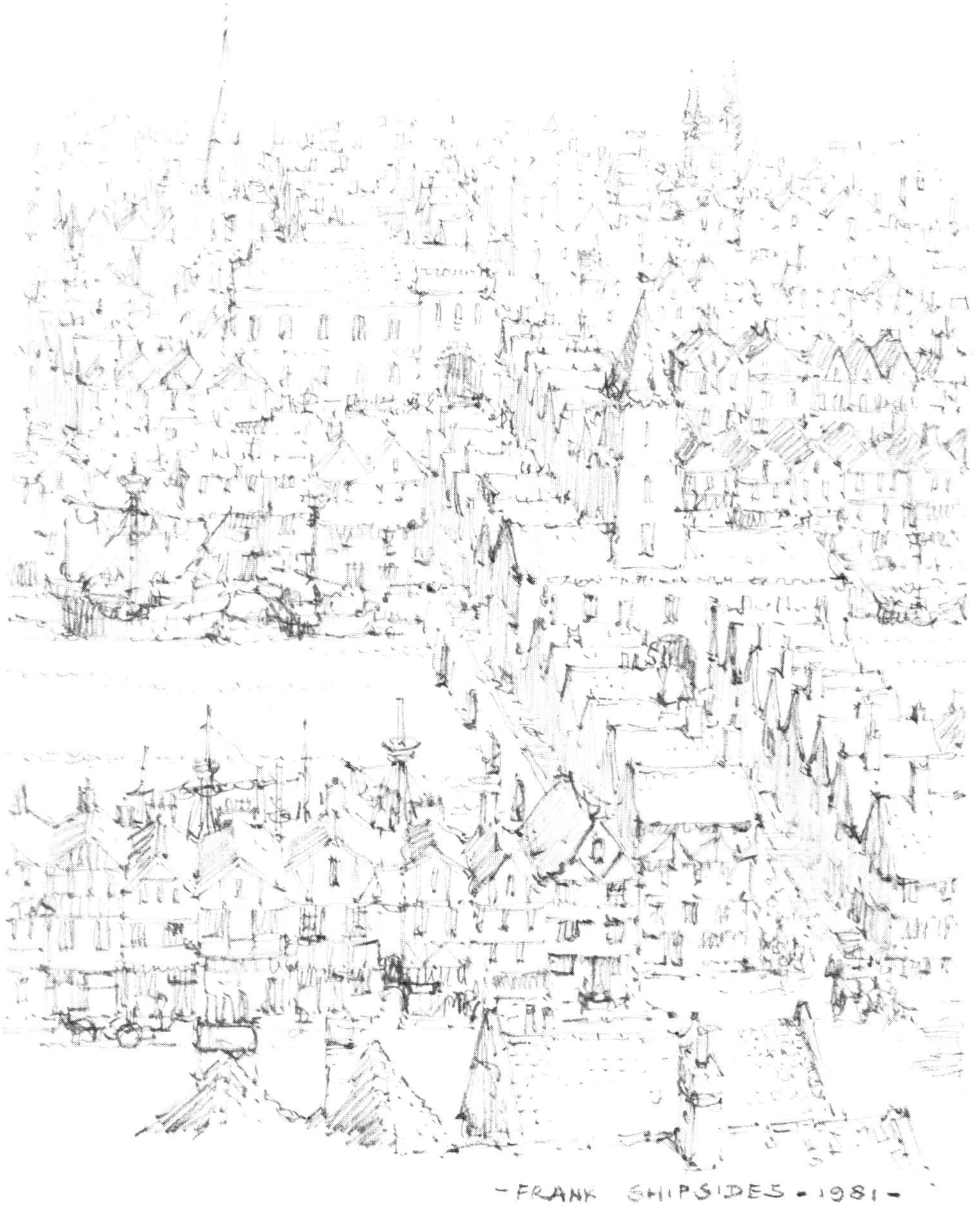

Old Bristol Bridge as it appeared from 1249 to 1762. The chapel in the centre was dedicated to Our Lady. The Bridge replaced an earlier wooden structure.

fishing voyages to the Newfoundland Banks, we are certain that Cabot sighted the mainland of North America on June 24th, 1497, the first European to do so in modern history. Cabot had left Bristol on May 2nd, but in one ship, the *Matthew* of fifty tons, with a crew of around twenty men. His son Sebastian claimed in later life that he was on board. This may be so. He was about fourteen at the time and would be considered mature. The outward voyage took thirty-five days in mostly fair weather. There is no evidence to pinpoint the landing place and it could have been anywhere from Maine to Labrador. Newfoundland has been the popular choice for Bristol historians. This was the second of John Cabot's voyages from Bristol. The first, abandoned for shortage of supplies, has been put at 1495. The Cabots (for history generally credits both father and son with the voyage) returned to Bristol in triumph on August 6th, 1497, after making their European landfall on the Brittany coast. Cabot, now an important national figure, confirmed the existence of the great cod fishing grounds off the coast of the 'new founde lande' and immediately set about preparations for a further voyage. As was to be expected, there was no lack of backers, but it seems that only one ship returned from the venture of the four that set out. John Cabot appears to have been lost at sea in 1498, and either Sebastian was not with him or survived in the ship that returned.

Where one Bristol ship could go, others soon followed. The names of Robert Thorne, the merchant who founded Bristol Grammar School, his brother Nicholas and their father, another Robert, are all linked with early Bristol trade with the west. The elder Thorne is said to have been a backer of Cabot and in 1527 the younger Robert claimed in a letter to King Henry VIII that 'my father which with another merchant of Bristowe named Hugh Eliot, were the discoverers of new founde landes . . .'.

There were annual voyages from Bristol to America commencing in 1501 by a group of men, of whom Asshehurst, John Thomas and Warde were prominent. These expeditions continued until 1506. Then, in 1508–9, Sebastian Cabot led a squadron of two ships in an attempt to find a north-west passage to the east. He failed but his course led him the whole span of the eastern seaboard of North America from Baffin Island to Florida. He returned to find that Henry VII had died in his absence and the new king, Henry VIII was actively discouraging exploration for fear of displeasing Spain, one of whose princesses, Catherine of Aragon, was his wife.

Sebastian Cabot severed his ties with Bristol this same year and moved to Spain.

The early voyages of discovery did not profit Bristol a great deal and there was little done by Englishmen in the first half of the sixteenth century to follow up and exploit Cabot's initiative. Individual Bristolians took ship with other nations and one of them, Master Andrew, sailed with Magellan on his 1519 circumnavigation. He died on the voyage, as did his admiral. While England paused, Spain and Portugal imposed their grip on the Americas.

Nevertheless, the door was open and the great days of the Elizabethans were at hand. In the time of Cabot, the Collector of Customs of the Port of Bristol was one Richard ap Meryk, or Ameryk. Staunchly, Bristolians claim that Cabot called his discovery America in the Collector's honour. It could well be so.

'The lusty ship of Bristol sailed out adventurously,
Against the foes of England their strength with them to try;
Well victual'd, rig'd, and man'd, and good provisioned still,
Which made them cry "To sea with the Angel Gabriel".'

Anon.—*the Ballad of the Angel Gabriel.*

Visit of Queen Elizabeth I in 1574.

For Queen, King and Parliament

THE YEARS of the intermediate Tudor monarchs, Henry VIII and his son and elder daughter, Edward VI and Mary I, lasted until 1558. They were indifferent times for the port of Bristol. Towards the end of his life, Sebastian Cabot returned to live in England and tried to interest the Bristol merchants in his company to trade with China but little came of it. Cabot died in 1557. Meanwhile, the controversies of the Reformation had broken out in England and all Bristol's religious houses vanished in the three years between 1536 and 1539. Standing across the marsh from the town, the Abbey of Saint Augustine survived to become the cathedral church of Bristol, one of five new dioceses that Henry VIII set up with the spoils of the Abbey. In a charter of 1542, Henry made Bristol a city, 169 years after she became a county, but the incoming Bishop Bush found his cathedral half demolished. Religious quarrels and persecutions would go on for nearly two centuries and Bristol would suffer with the rest of England, but the reign of Elizabeth I which started in 1558 was a tolerant interlude and Bristol benefited accordingly.

Bristol ships and seamen served Henry VIII well, and Sir Robert Poyntz of Iron Acton was such a one. He was Chancellor to Queen Catherine of Aragon and accompanied Henry to the Field of the Cloth of Gold in 1520. He is buried in the Lord Mayor's Chapel, dying in 1521. Antony, son of

Sir Robert, was Captain of the *Trinity,* one of four Bristol ships provided for the King in 1513. Their Admiral, Sir John Howard wrote to the King:

> 'Sir, the shipps of Bristowe be her with me, I assur Your Gras, gorgeas shipps for their burdon. . . . I understand they lak vital. . . .'

Three of the Bristol ships were in action in Bertheaume Bay, where Howard was killed boarding a French flagship. Later in the reign, a contemporary manuscript mentions 'the great services done to King Henry VIII by Bristowe in the wars against the French king . . . at which this town did set forth eight ships. When King Henry VIII came on board Bristowe's fleet on that memorable time, he asked the names of their ships. . . .'

Henry VIII died in 1547 and his son, the sickly Edward VI started his brief six years on the throne. Yet Bristol cherishes his memory, for he it was who in 1552, in response to a petition from the Bristol merchants about the run down state of their port, issued letters patent on December 18th of that year which incorporated 'in one bodye and one Comynaltie Corporated forever by the name of the Maister, Wardeins and Comynaltie of the merchant venturers of the City of Bristol'. So began the formal history of the great Society of Merchant Venturers, which for the next two and a half centuries was to exercise such important and decisive influence on the development of England's trade, and, as Charles McInnes rightly claimed, on her empire as well. Certainly one of the greatest of all trade guilds, the first Master was one of the petitioners, Edward Prin, or Prynne, and the meetings were held in the old chapel of St. Clement near the Broad Quay, which became the Merchants Hall. It was subsequently rebuilt in 1787 and served until its destruction in the German air raids of 1940 and 1941. Today Merchants Hall is located in a careful conversion of two houses, Fern House and Auckland House, Clifton, appropriately just a few yards from the Mansion House.

The many services of the Society to its fellow citizens in the promotion of trade, building, commerce, education at all levels, social welfare and security and all manner of charity has been told by Professor McGrath in *The Merchant Venturers of Bristol,* to which the interested reader is recommended. The immediate effect of the charter was to bar foreign trade in and out of Bristol to all but the members of the Society, nor can it be gainsaid that this meant only the richer citizens and their sons. Yet the arrangement was appropriate to the age, where the physical dangers of trade were immense, and required the careful skill and sensible judgment that the Bristol merchants had acquired by long and often painful experience.

The Castle moat is the last remaining large relic of Bristol Castle which was begun c. 1070 and demolished in 1665.

By the reign of Elizabeth I, the population of the merchant city had risen to 6,000 although it was still largely contained within the old walls. The peace that followed the Wars of the Roses encouraged some building outside however, and larger houses began to appear along St. Augustines Back and up the Kingsdown slopes. Trade was, nevertheless, depressed due to the worsening relationship with Spain that followed the Reformation, and Bristol shipping was hard hit. An example of Bristol privateers hitting back occurred in 1575 when the ship *Christopher* belonging to Andrew Barker of Bristol was seized in Tenerife. Barker replied by fitting out the *Bear* and the *Ragged Staff* with which he proceeded to pillage along the Spanish Main until disagreements with his crew led to his being marooned. He was killed by the Spaniards. Both the ships were lost and the survivors returned in a captured frigate, only to be prosecuted for their disloyalty to Barker.

At this time also, the Bristol merchants had an interest in the attempts by Sir Martin Frobisher to discover the elusive North–West Passage in his expeditions of 1576, 1577 and 1578. Among these were Sir William Wynter and his brother George, who also partly financed Drake's famous circumnavigation of 1577–80. The family sent Captain John Wynter with the fleet in the *Elizabeth* to watch their interests. John Wynter is a controversial figure who has been accused of deserting Drake when the *Elizabeth* turned back near the Straits of Magellan. Others argue that this was against his wishes but his crew would sail no farther.

In 1574, Queen Elizabeth made her celebrated visit to Bristol. She had been expected in 1570 and the Council had gone to some expense in a panic owing to their long neglect of the city's road surfaces. Then the Queen changed the route of her 'progress'. However, her 1574 visit was announced and one of Bristol's first supplementary rates raised £535. 1s. 7d. The Council borrowed another £450 (literally from the poor box!) and the Dean and Chapter put up another £5. The Queen arrived on August 14th and was greeted by the Mayor and Common Council, and after lengthy speeches, Her Majesty then went in procession to the High Cross, newly re-gilded for the visit, and then on to the new Great House of Mr. John Young on St. Augustines Back (later to become Colston's School) where she was to stay a week, in the process knighting her host and pardoning nine prisoners condemned to death and lying in Newgate.

Elizabeth's visit was notable for a trip she made at the end of the week down the Avon to Kingroad to review Bristol's shipping. The party travelled in three decorated galleys and the sight must have been one of the great set pieces of Bristol's history. The river has been the scene of many famous passages but few can have outdone for pageantry that day in the summer of 1574 when England's greatest ruler passed down the Avon.

The bitter argument with Spain broke into open conflict in 1585 which sharpened in 1587 with the execution of the Catholic claimant to the throne, Mary of Scotland, and Phillip II determined on the plan to dispatch his great Armada. It is surprising that, considering she was able to put twenty-four ships for Edward III in 1346, Bristol sent only four to the fleet gathering in Plymouth to confront the Duke of Medina-Sidonia. Of course, the *Unicorn, Minion, Handmaid* and *Aid* were larger vessels, but the small number may in truth reflect the depressed state of the port that led to the charter to the Society of Merchant Venturers in 1552. The spirit of the time is well captured by Macaulay who, in *The Armada,* writes of the English reaction to the arrival of the Spanish fleet off the Lizard:—

> 'Right sharp and quick the bells all night rang out from Bristol town
> And 'ere the day three hundred horse had met on Clifton Down.'

and later:

> 'Night sank upon the dusky beach and on the purple sea,
> Such night in England n'er had been, nor e'er again shall be.'

The reality was somewhat different, but it was true that there was great excitement in the city. The Bristol ships had sailed three months earlier in April and the city's trained bands had been drilled constantly since Lady Day, but news from the fleet was sparse and it was not until August 4th that news arrived of the defeat of the Armada in Calais Roads. Great rejoicing broke out in the streets.

For the historian, the most important name of Elizabethan Bristol must be that of Richard Hakluyt, the writer and thinker who spent his time in persuading his countrymen of the benefits of further colonisation. The failure of Gilbert's Newfoundland venture, in which Bristol had a share, and his loss on the *Squirrel* in 1579, only spurred Hakluyt on to greater

The Broad Quay by St. Stephen's Church.

effort and his *Navigations, Voyages and Discoveries of the English Nation,* first published in 1582, was an inspiration to his fellows. Hakluyt settled in Bristol in 1585 and from his writing sprang some of the city's early voyages to the coasts of New England and Canada in the opening years of the seventeenth century.

The Llandoger Trow Inn, dating from 1669, provides today's Bristolians with a picture of the appearance of the City in Stuart times.

Queen Elizabeth died in 1603. Earlier, in 1601, she had said 'Though God has raised me high, yet this I count the glory of my crown; that I have ruled with your loves'. Now her love affair with the English people was over and a very different kind of ruler sat on the chair of St. Edward. James I did not share Elizabeth's skill in winning the hearts and minds of his subjects. Hence they could always respond to her demands for money, knowing that her frugal parsimony would ensure careful public spending. They placed no such trust in the Stuarts and Bristol fell out with James almost from the first days of his reign.

Paradoxically, these were the years that Bristol turned to colonisation, the rooting of English settlements principally in Virginia, as the general area south of 45 degrees north latitude had come to be called. Encouraged by Hakluyt, Robert Aldworth and John Whitson fitted out the *Speedwell* and the *Discoverer* for a voyage in 1603, under the command of Martin Pring, having first obtained the sanction of Sir Walter Raleigh, the Royal concession holder for Virginia. Pring sailed from Kingroad on March

20th, 1603, and eventually entered a bay which he named after Whitson. Seventeen years later, Captain Christopher Jones of the *Mayflower* landed the Pilgrims in the same spot and the bay became Plymouth Harbour thereafter. Pring stayed seven weeks trading with local Indians and scaring them away with two mastiffs he had on board. He returned to Bristol on October 2nd, with an Indian canoe and a story of a country 'full of God's good blessings'.

Aldworth and Whitson are two of Bristol's most famous names. The former established the first sugar trade in the city, helped with the restoration of the Society of Merchant Venturers in 1605/6 after its influence had faded towards the end of the sixteenth century, and was the founder of the first town in New England to be called Bristol. This was in 1632, and today there are twenty-two other Bristols in the U.S.A. Whitson is usually considered the archetypal Bristol merchant venturer and something of a legend. Born in 1555 in the Forest of Dean, he managed to overcome the strict entrance rules of the Society of Merchant Venturers, which insisted that only sons of members or apprentices (an expensive undertaking) could enrol in that select band of 100 or so merchants. Whitson enhanced his prospects by marrying the widow of his late employer. That bawdy raconteur John Aubrey has a hilarious account of the good lady being seduced by Whitson in the cellar. Aubrey was Whitson's godson and this alone ought to have made him sure of his facts.

By the time of the new king, Whitson was one of Bristol's most influential men. He was a councillor, became Mayor and M.P. and took part in the first arguments that were to lead up to the Civil War. Whitson died on March 9th, 1629, leaving many charitable bequests, of which one was the foundation of Red Maids School.

Martin Pring was back in America in 1606, the real leader of two ships under the command of Thomas Hanham, which had been fitted out by Sir John Popham, Chief Justice and Sir Ferdinando Gorges of Wraxall Court, near Bristol and military commander at Plymouth. Gorges was a persistent coloniser whose fortunes varied over the years but he is credited with the foundation of the State of Maine. Later in life, he married the widow of one of the Smyths of Ashton Court and he died there at the age of eighty-two in 1647, after a loyal service to Charles I in the Civil War. Pring voyaged much in later years in Asian waters and is buried in St.

Stephens Churchyard, Bristol, where he died in 1627. His monument is in the church.

James I was hardly on the throne before he began to collect money by imposing customs duty on goods not approved by Parliament. This led to Whitson, at the time Mayor, declaring such duties illegal. Bristol protested and the House of Commons petitioned the King. Resistance proved futile and the King's agents ranged through the city, taking the goods of those who refused to pay. Later James began granting monopolies in certain trades. Two of these, smokers' pipes and starch, were granted to Londoners. Both trades were active in Bristol and their owners were deprived of the work. The haughty and untrustworthy Charles I succeeded his father in 1625 and matters grew worse. In 1631 London was given the monopoly in soap making, a long standing Bristol industry, and Bristol soap merchants faced ruin. Some of the wealthier merchants were able to benefit from these monopolies, and this probably explains their support for the King in the approaching war, while small traders were all for the Parliamentary cause.

War with Spain in 1625 and France in 1627 brought defeat to England at Cadiz and La Rochelle. Ten Bristol ships were provided under pressure from the Duke of Buckingham, but the most famous exploit was that of the Bristol privateer *Angel Gabriel,* 280 tons, under Captain Netheway, which beat off three Spanish ships in a seven hour fight, killing 500 for the loss of three Bristol men. The fight was celebrated in the ballad 'The Honour of Bristol'.

Peace came in 1630 and the following year Captain Thomas James set out from Bristol to once more seek the elusive North–West Passage. The Society sponsored the voyage and James left the port on May 3rd in the *Henrietta Maria,* 70 tons, named in honour of the Queen. This followed an audience that Charles had granted Captain James before his sailing. James entered Hudson Bay by July 16th but could not find a passage to the north. He had nearly lost his ship on the Greenland coast and grounded once again on the west coast of the Bay. Here he met up with a London ship, the *Charles,* Captain Foxe.

There was no love lost between the two men. Foxe was a professional seaman while James had started life as a lawyer. Foxe returned to England but James stayed on to winter in Canada and returned to Bristol in

October 1632. His adventures had included sinking his ship for the winter to avoid her being crushed in the ice. She was in a most unseaworthy state when she returned to Bristol, but James had laid the foundations of the lucrative fur trade. He became a naval officer but died in 1635. MacInnes says that he is buried in an unmarked grave in the Lord Mayor's Chapel.

Charles I continued the provocation of Bristol merchants in 1631 by banning the tobacco trade, but the earlier imposition of Ship Money dues in 1626 became one of the main causes of the Civil War. Charles argued that a standing navy was necessary for the defence of the country. He was right in this view but his subjects suspected that this was only a device to obtain money that had been denied him by Parliament. Bristol was charged £2,400 and the merchants were outraged. By 1634, the tax was running at about £1,000 annually and in this same year Archbishop Laud was in Bristol, reminding the city of the persecution the Established church was handing out to the Puritans, of which Bristol had many.

The long forecast war between the King and Parliament opened in 1642. It was essentially a land war, as most civil fights are, and the story of the city's adherence to Parliament, its capture by Prince Rupert in July 1643 and his subsequent loss of his prize to Fairfax and Cromwell in September 1645 have all been well recorded. The maritime events of the war are few. Parliamentary ships blockaded the Avon in 1645, and the great Admiral Robert Blake, born at Bridgwater in 1599, began his military career as a soldier of fortune in the defence of the city in 1643. During the Royalist occupation, the trade of the city almost vanished and a decade of hard work during the Commonwealth was needed for its recovery. Again the way lay across the western oceans, to the islands of the West Indies. By the time of the Restoration of Charles II in 1660, Bristol was prosperous again. Samuel Pepys' visit here in 1668 is dealt with in Chapter 7—in his experienced eyes the port was a 'large and noble place'.

Charles II had a soft spot for Bristol as he had been helped to escape through the city after his defeat at the Battle of Worcester. He returned as King in 1663 and stayed a day. Prince Rupert was with him and the royal party sampled Bristol Milk and attended a banquet. Also present were the Duke of York (later James II) and the ill-fated Duke of Monmouth.

One Bristolian who had cause to be grateful to the restored King was Admiral Sir William Penn (1621–70), whose father Giles was a Bristol merchant. He fought for the Parliament in the Civil War and by the First Dutch War, he was a vice-admiral and second in command to Blake. He offered in 1654 to take the fleet over to Charles II, but withdrew the offer when he was appointed by Cromwell to lead a squadron to capture Hispaniola, a venture that failed but ended with the taking of Jamaica. Penn fell into disfavour and retired to an Irish estate awarded him from dispossessed Royalists, from which he emerged to help in the Restoration of 1660. He was rewarded by being made a Commissioner of the Navy, and saw action at the battle off Lowestoft in 1665. Penn was buried at St. Mary Redcliffe.

His son, William Penn, angered his father by joining the Quakers, the pacifist sect founded by George Fox, and the victims of much persecution in the last half of the seventeenth century. In 1667 the Quakers felt strong enough to build their own meeting room in the garden of the old Dominican Friary, which they later acquired to beget the name Quakers Friars. When Admiral Penn died, the King owed him large arrears of salary. These were settled in 1681 by a grant of 47,000 acres of land in America. Penn the Younger used his share for the great experiment in political, social and religious freedom that became Pennsylvania.

Bristol was held for the King by the Duke of Beaufort during the Monmouth Rising against James II in June 1685. The citizens were inclined to Monmouth, who actually got as far as Keynsham, but Beaufort's hold on the city probably saved many necks when Judge Jeffreys held an assize here after Monmouth's defeat and execution. It was on this visit that Jeffreys rightly berated the Mayor and Council for their involvement in the slave trade. 'Kidnapper!' the Lord Chief Justice roared at the unfortunate Chief citizen. It is no small wonder that Bristol declared promptly for William of Orange in 1688. The flight of James II marked the end of the old Bristol. True the city was much the same as ever, largely enclosed in its walls. But the castle, symbol of so much strife and repression, had been demolished in 1655 and its fall coincided with the birth of new ideas about social justice. The men of Bristol had taken these ideas with them to the colonies in the New World and would eventually develop the passion for freedom that inspired Washington's armies and led to the foundation of the United States.

Looking towards Hotwells.

RANK SHIPSIDES - 1981

ARIGUANI
FRANK SHIPSIDES 1981

The coat of arms of the City and County of Bristol. The ship and castle date from a seal of 1350.

Elders & Fyffes Ariguani *leaving Avonmouth.*

'The streaky Severn changes on the sight,
Waving to beams of many colour'd light;
O'er the clear main dispers'd, the less'ning sail,
(Thy wealth, proud Bristol!) dances in the gale.'

Thomas Hobhouse—*Kingsweston Hill, 1785.*

A Bristol Privateer in action.

Privateers, Pirates and Profits

AT THE beginning of the eighteenth century, Bristol entered on what some writers have described as her Golden Age. The phrase is a hackneyed one, but apt, for in no previous time in her history had the wealth of her citizens been so extensive. She was Britain's leading port after London and would remain so for most of the century. Her population was 20,000 in 1700 and would grow another 44,000 by the century's end. The remains of the eighteenth century expansion can be seen in Bristol today in such buildings as the Corn Exchange, the houses of Orchard Street and St. Thomas Church. Park Street was laid out and on the Marsh, behind the quays and shipyards, the well ordered grace of Queen's Square took shape to become one of Bristol's glories. As the century ended, Clifton had started the climb along her gorge that was to lift the suburb to the heights of Georgian elegance.

All these changes from a medieval town to a modern European city were funded by the great leap forward in trade which began in the last years of the seventeenth century and led to the development of new markets in Virginia, the Carolinas and the West Indies. As a measure of Bristol's trade, the following statistics are enlightening: In 1687, 240 ships sailed from the Avon, by 1787 the figure was 448, while foreign port arrivals were 238 and 485 respectively. But the ships of 1787 were on average a third larger, so it is fairly safe to argue that the trade of the port trebled in size during these years. Meanwhile the traditional trades with Ireland, the Baltic and France continued as strongly as before.

Rum, sugar and tobacco were Bristol's principal American imports and to these was added the controversial and loathsome slaving. In 1698 Parliament broke the monopoly of the Royal African Company and made trade to that continent open to all who paid ten per cent on all traded goods in or out, except redwood five per cent and gold, silver and negroes, which were free! Bristol merchants had been aware of the possibilities of the trade for decades. There was a huge demand for labour in the plantations of the Americas and the Dutch were supplying the colonists as early as the time of the Civil War. In 1694, there was a petition to Parliament from the city, because although 10,000 indentured white servants had sailed through Bristol for the Indies between 1654–85, they were unsuited for work in the tropics and died off like flies. Negro labour was far superior. To get the slave trade opened to Bristolians, a campaign was organised by the Society of Merchant Venturers.

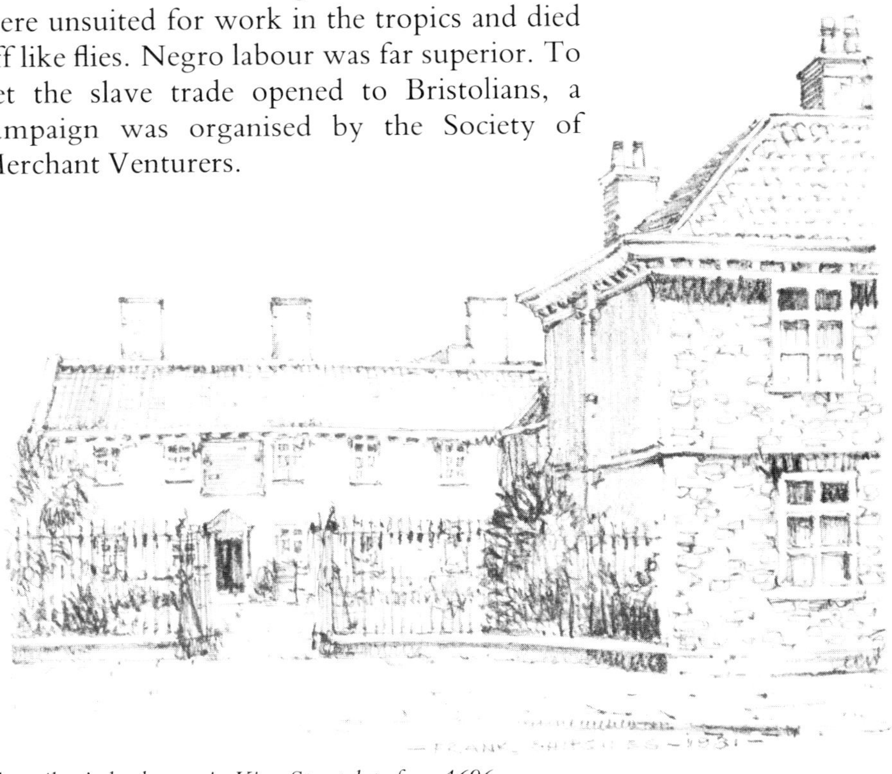

The sailors' almshouses in King Street date from 1696.

Fitting out the Duke *and the* Duchess *in Bristol in the spring of 1708 for Captain Woodes Rogers' expedition.*

The Society was dissatisfied with the Act which cost it ten per cent on its trade goods, while at the same time it had to fight off the demands of the Royal African Company for the return of its monopoly. The squabble went on for over half a century until the trade was regulated in 1750 by Bristol becoming a full partner in the new company of merchants trading to Africa. Despite all her complaints, Bristol grew rich on the slave trade. In the first decade of the century, an average of fifty ships a year sailed from the city to the Guinea coast and in 1725, Bristol ships carried 16,950 slaves to American ports. Nevertheless, the figures over the century as a whole show that London and Liverpool were far greater slavers than Bristol ever was. As an example, in the ten years 1795–1804, Bristol transported 10,718 negro slaves, while London's total was 46,405 and Liverpool's an incredible 332,800! This was while the abolition campaign was gathering momentum.

Conditions in the slave ships were appalling, as the vessels were usually very small compared to other traders. Up to 300 people would be crammed into a ninety ton vessel. The slave ship had to be fast, in order to stand some chance of delivering its cargo in reasonable condition. The trade on the coast was risky, lawlessness abounded and the risk of epidemic was constant. But treble profits could come from a voyage—on the cloth, powder, shot, pistols, beads and other artifacts exchanged with local chieftains for the slaves; on the slaves themselves, and on the sugar and rum sold in Bristol on the ship's return to the city. The one thing not sold was the grim collection of leg-irons, chains, manacles and whips that were the slaver's trade mark. Many leading Bristolians, all upright men, took part in the trade. One slave ship, the privateer *Southwell,* 400 tons and twenty-four guns, was named after a Bristol M.P. She arrived in Antigua in October, 1746, having lost 150 slaves on the voyage but still had 301 available for the auctioneer. Depending on sex and condition, at that time they may have sold for an average of £30 a piece.

Another activity of eighteenth century Bristol was privateering. England fought six major wars in the course of the century and Bristol privateers were active in all of them. When the War of the Spanish Succession broke out in 1702, 127 private ships of war were equipped and sent out from the city before the peace treaty was signed at Utrecht in April, 1713. In a way, privateering was an industry, as the objective was spoil gained from the enemy and the Bristol merchants joined in with enthusiasm. Even some of the Quakers were reportedly involved, according to Damar Powell.

To this war, which contained Marlborough's brilliant Continental campaigns, Bristol owes the story of its most famous privateering voyage. A proclamation of June 1st, 1702, awarded any prize taken to the owners and crew of the privateer, except for Customs duties and ten per cent to the Crown. This may have encouraged a certain Captain Woodes Rogers to propose to a group of Bristol merchants a voyage to the Pacific for the purpose of privateering in the seas that Spain considered her own private lake. Woodes Rogers hailed from Poole where he had been born in 1679 and he had married the daughter of a prominent Bristolian. His idea was supported and two ships, the *Duke* and the *Duchess* were fitted out. Both were 300 tons but the *Duke* carried thirty guns to the twenty-four of the *Duchess,* according to Damar Powell. Rogers' own account rates the *Duke* as only twenty guns. This may well be a misprint, as Rogers' book has been republished several times.

The ships left Bristol on August 1st, 1708, and sailed via Cork to pick up additional crew. With Rogers in the *Duke* was Captain William Dampier of East Coker, Somerset, who had already been twice around the world in a lively career of seaman, buccaneer and navigator. It was his brilliance in the latter capacity and his knowledge of the South Sea that earned his place on the voyage. A few prizes of no exceptional value were taken on the way south and the Horn was rounded on January 11th, 1709. Rogers gives his farthest south as sixty-one degrees fifty-three minutes. He then made for the island of Juan Fernandez to refit, rest and take on fresh water. He arrived on February 1st and that night was alarmed to see a light on the island, supposing it came from a Spanish garrison. The next day he was greeted by Alexander Selkirk, a Scots seaman who had been marooned on Juan Fernandez four years earlier by Captain Stradling of the privateer *Cinque-Ports.* Selkirk had survived quite easily, living off the goats and vegetables which abounded on the island. Selkirk knew Dampier who had sailed as Captain of the *St. George* in the same expedition as Stradling, but the ships had parted company early in the voyage. The castaway had no great opinion of his former officer and had to be persuaded with some difficulty to leave his island home.

Rogers and his fleet left Juan Fernandez on February 13th and carried out a successful campaign off the coasts of Panama and Mexico. They captured several ships and then made for Peru where a raid was made on Guayaquil on April 23rd. It was not until December that the privateers came up with their main objective, the annual Manila galleons. They took the treasure ship *Nuestra Señora de la Encarnacion Desengano,* Rogers being wounded in the action, and came up with the second ship, the *Bigonia* in the early hours of Christmas Day. In a running fight over two days, the *Bigonia* beat them off and Rogers then determined it was time to return to England. This he did by sailing across the Pacific via Guam to avoid the now thoroughly aroused Spaniards, and arrived in the Texel from the Cape of Good Hope on July 23rd, 1711. The cruise had netted £148,000 and was one of the most remarkable voyages by an Englishman up to that time, while the story of Selkirk inspired Defoe's *Robinson Crusoe.*

On his return, Rogers lived with his family in Queen Square, as befitted his success. Two silver candlesticks still remain in Bristol Cathedral as a memorial of his voyage. He later spent two successful terms as a popular Governor of the Bahamas and died in Nassau on July 15th, 1732.

A typical slaver of the early nineteenth century, the Nymph *(1820) captured by the Royal Navy in 1831.*

This epic of Woodes Rogers was Bristol's most rewarding privateering adventure. She continued to supply ships for the purpose until the system ended towards the end of the Georgian era. Not always was cruising so profitable, particularly in the War of American Independence (1775–83) when all save two or three Bristol privateers 'sustained disastrous losses', according to Latimer. Only one prize of any consequence was brought into the city, and the most notable action was that of Captain John Shaw of Shirehampton, in the *Lion* and the *Vigilant,* who fought off two French battleships of three times his strength, in an action in the Bay of Biscay. Bristol's sympathies were very much with the colonists at this time. She had close ties with the emerging United States, and one of her M.Ps, the orator Edmund Burke, argued the American cause sympathetically. But Bristol still supplied 157 privateers for the war. After that, the enthusiasm seems to lapse, for only sixty-three Bristol ships served as privateers through the whole twenty-two years of the war against Napoleon.

Bristol trade was at its best in the early years of the century and the merchants at their richest. Ironically, the philanthropist, Tory and High Churchman Edward Colston, one of Bristol's most revered sons, made most of his fortune trading in London, only returning to Bristol to dispense it to many charities, endow education in the schools that bear his named and die in 1721 to become posthumously the most celebrated merchant and citizen in the city's long history.

As always in the history of the port, the Avon continued to exert its capricious tidal influence on dock affairs and it is to the docks and riverside that we must now return. As early as the 1620s, Robert Aldworth had opened Bristol's first private dock but the great desire of any shipper using Bristol was for a wet dock where a ship could always float at any state of the tide. Ships could only keep afloat as far up the river as Hungroad and here all the timber from the Baltic was put over the side in barges. Since 1662, the size of ships coming up river had been strictly controlled and all required a pass issued at Hungroad. From here the hobblers took over and an average ship needed nine boats and three dozen oarsmen to tow her to Broad Quay. To overcome some of these problems, a group of merchants led by Joshua Franklin, in 1712 started the construction of a wet dock at Sea Mills on the north bank of the river. The work was completed in 1717 but was never really successful, as the road to Bristol was bad and the traders considered the dock lay too far from the city. It was used by privateers and a whaling company in mid-century, but had been abandoned by 1779.

In 1765, another attempt to beat the tide was made. William Champion built a large wet dock capable of serving thirty-six ships and placed two graving docks alongside. But Champion ran out of money, and in 1770 sold his property to the Society of Merchant Venturers. It was thereafter known as Merchants Dock. The Society found it a mixed blessing and expensive to operate. So under the guise of concern with fire precautions, they promoted an Act of Parliament which gave their dock a monopoly of the timber wharfage, which outraged the trade. Still, the Society did quite well in other parts of the port, and made large sums from the supply of cranes. In 1764 their concession was renewed by the Common Council in return for extensions of the quays at Welsh Back and St. Augustine's Reach and a new quay at the Grove.

But large as her trade was, Bristol had been overtaken by Liverpool as the second port of Britain by mid-century and, equally important, the size of ships was increasing to a point where it would be impossibly dangerous for them to use the Avon. This threat of ever larger ships would loom again in 1890 and 1960!

If Bristol were to halt the trade losses, then she would have to be able to accept the larger ships. In 1758, the Council advertised for consulting engineers but an effort to raise money for a floating dock scheme found few subscribers. The engineer Smeaton was brought in—he of the Eddystone Lighthouse—and William Champion offered his dockbuilding experience, but the Council found all schemes too costly for their pocket. The matter rested for over twenty years until a survey by the engineer Nickalls in 1787, who proposed a dam in the Avon at Black Rock. Smeaton was on the scene again in 1790 but nothing was done. By now the situation was getting urgent. The harnessing of steam and the discovery of plentiful coal fields in the North had set off the industrial revolution and a frenzy of new factory building. Bristol's trade declined further in proportion to the national total and long established trades began to leave the city. Then, against fierce Bristol opposition, William Wilberforce was making steady progress in his campaign to ban the Slave Trade and would succeed by 1807. The French Wars also added to the decline.

The frigate Melampus, *built at Albion Dockyard in 1785.*

Looking towards Hungroad in the mid-eighteenth century.

By 1791, the Society were getting desperate, and forced a still reluctant Council to form a joint committee, but war with France lasted from 1793 until 1802. Then the decision was taken in the optimistic atmosphere of peace and a scheme commissioned from the foremost civil engineer, William Jessop. He dismissed all previous ideas and produced a plan that was substantially in the form of the present Floating Harbour. It was published in May, 1802, and the Bristol Dock Company was floated with a capital of £200,000. By the time the money had been raised, Jessop had suggested an improved plan which included all the city quays and left no option for a vessel to lie outside the harbour. This appealed very much and Jessop costed the works at £212,000 including all bridges. The entire cost was considered to be easily covered by £300,000.

Local shipowners complained that the scheme laid before Parliament in a Bill of 1802 forced them to use the facilities whether they wanted them or not, but the Royal assent was obtained on August 11th, 1803. The Dock Company was controlled by the Council and the Merchants acting as one, and, the contract having been let, the first sod was cut on May 1st, 1804 before a large crowd at 5 a.m.! The works involved a large new locked entrance at Hotwells, a new basin to be named after the Duke of

Cumberland, a New Cut for the River Avon, three dams, a Feeder Canal, and Bath and Bedminster Bridges. Inevitably, the work cost more than the estimate and the final bill was for £600,000, largely due to inflation caused by the war renewed with France in 1803. Bristol had her modern port, however, and it was now up to her what use she made of it. In January 1809, water was let into the New Cut for the first time. The nineteenth century could begin.

'I'm the Queen of the Waters—the ocean world
Has never yet seen a sail unfurl'd
Like mine o'er its billowing heaving breast,
Or the sea-bird that carried a prouder crest!'

Lines from *The Times,* 1845

s.s. Great Britain *at sea.*

Port Imperial—The Port of Bristol in the Nineteenth Century

As THE Floating Harbour opened its new lock gates to shipping in the spring of 1809, the Directors of the Dock Company sat back to examine the position of their new enterprise and they derived little encouragement from the results. The heady days of debate, excavation and royal visits were over, the civic banquets were eaten, the speeches made and the toasts all drunk. The guests had departed and the directors now found themselves faced with making the dock work and, in most people's eyes, more important, making it pay. The shareholders had been given frequent promises of substantial dividends and now expected the promises to be fulfilled. Furthermore, many of them were looking for repayment of the loan capital in full.

The expectations were in vain. The doubling in price of the original contract for the harbour works had loaded the Company with an impossible burden, and the expectations of the city's investors made an already bad situation worse. The dues raised on shipping entering the port soared to become the highest of any charged in major British ports. Shipping companies looked elsewhere and Liverpool benefited above all others. On top went the Town dues charged by the Corporation and these were equally exorbitant. So there were the Society, the Council and the Company, all three in the hands of mostly the same people, forcing up the port charges, instead of trying to create a competitive situation *vis-a-vis* other ports. Charges were forty-eight per cent above those in Liverpool and 115 per cent in London. Yet a dividend was not paid until 1823.

The ending of the slave trade in 1807 had been followed in 1833 by the emancipation of all slaves in the West Indies, which caused a sharp rise in the cost of sugar, already put sky high in Bristol by the West India Company. Then duties on foreign sugar were removed and the sugar trade in the West Indies collapsed. In 1830, sixty-three per cent of Bristol trade was with the Carribbean; it had vanished by the nineties. As a distinguished past Secretary of the P.B.A. has written, the 1803 Act was 'an early masterpiece of legal and financial manipulation' whereby 'the Corporation and the Merchant Venturers had secured power without financial responsibility!'

There was the other problem of making the dock work. Here the Company was more successful. There were early problems such as landslips at Cumberland Basin and the collapse of Hill's Bridge in 1806 which were dealt with by the resident site engineer, Josias Jessop, who was the son of the designer of the dock system and who stayed on as consulting engineer until his death in 1827. Consultations were rare and there is some indication that this could have been due to the everlasting lack of money. More probably the dock was proving satisfactory in service.

One snag with the new dock was its smell. The locks at the entrance had stopped the twice daily tidal scour that had been Bristol's sewage disposal system since the foundation of the city. All the waste was allowed to enter the harbour which became akin to an open latrine for close on 100,000 people. The summer of 1825 was very hot and the harbour stank intolerably. The Dock Company refused to take action and so the Paving Commissioners went to court and obtained a *mandamus* to force it to do so. An engineer called Mylne built a conduit from the Frome right across the city to discharge into the New Cut. Of course this transferred the smell to Bedminster whose sturdy residents were somewhat upset, but they had to wait until the next century before the smell was finally removed.

The return of the s.s. Great Britain.

FRANK SHIPSIDES 1981

F. A. Ashmead & Son Ltd.

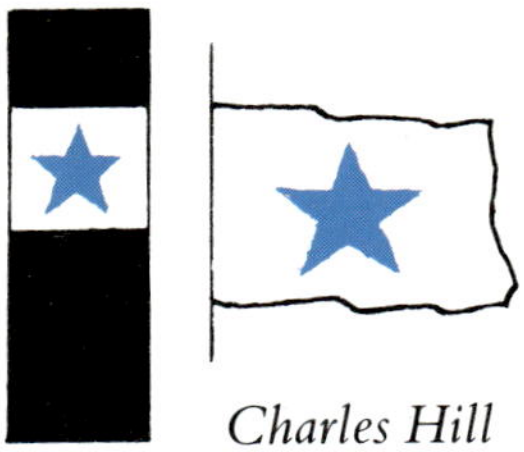
Charles Hill & Sons Ltd.

Rae Towing Co. Ltd.

Wm. Cory & Son Ltd.

Port of Bristol

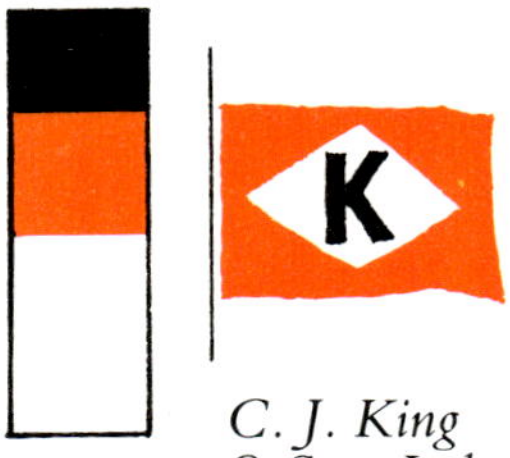
C. J. King & Sons Ltd.

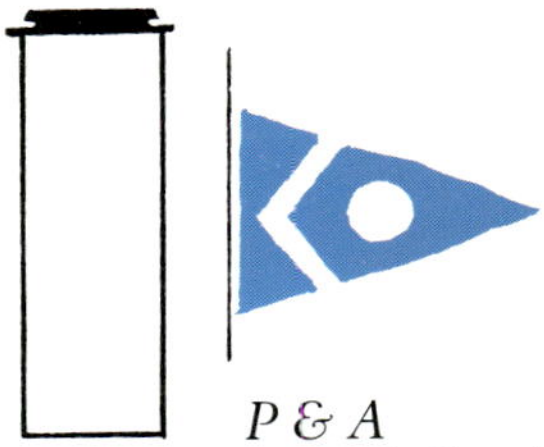
P & A Campbell Ltd.

T. R. Brown & Sons Ltd.

Bristol Steam Navigation Co. Ltd.

Osborne & Wallis Ltd.

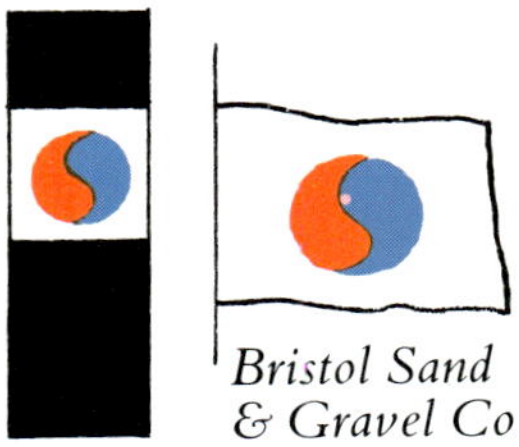
Bristol Sand & Gravel Co. Ltd.

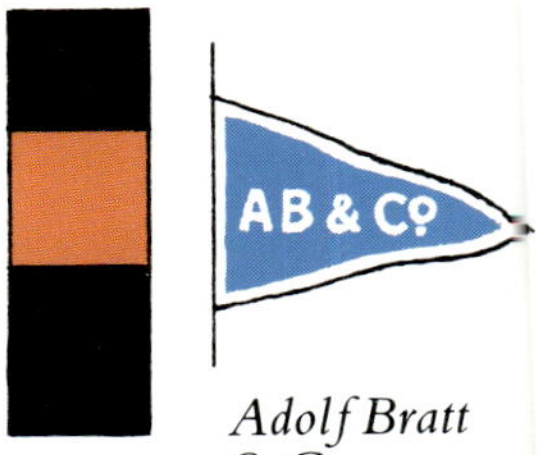
Adolf Bratt & Co.

Hollandsche Stoomboot Maatschappij

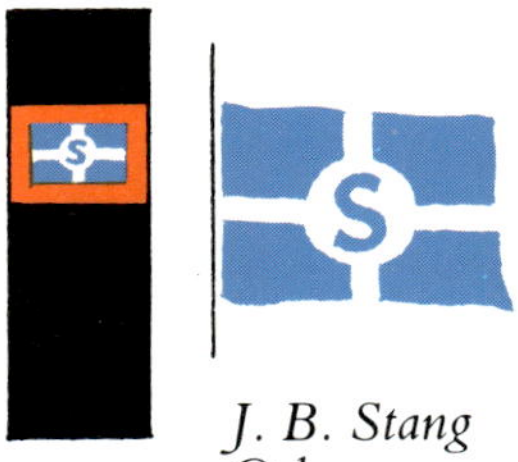
J. B. Stang Oslo

Sven Redig (Transmarin) Helsingborg

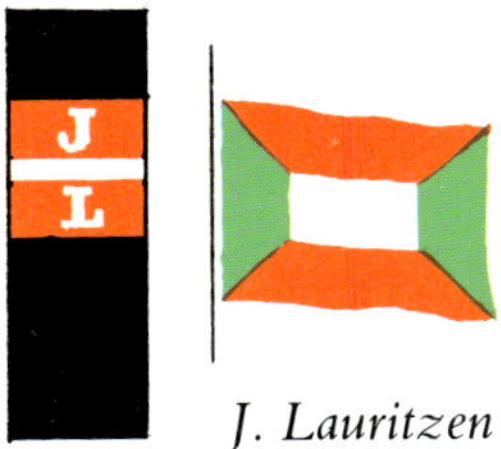
J. Lauritzen Copenhagen

Ald Shipping Co. (A. L. Duggan)

Coast Lines Ltd.

Elders & Fyffe Ltd.

Wm. Sloan & Co. Ltd.

Mark Whitwill & Son Ltd.

Blue Star Line Ltd.

Harrison Ltd.

Port Line Ltd.

Bristol Bridge in the early nineteenth century, based on an old print.

The next problems occurred in 1832, in the year when the city was recovering from the aftermath of the Bristol Riots of late October, 1831. The silting in the harbour was alarming and one of the directors recommended a young engineer who had recovered in Bristol from an accident, and had since spent two years here.

The directors may have had reservations about the youthfulness of their new consultant (he was twenty-six) but, they soon discovered that in Mr. I. K. Brunel they had an engineer of genius, and that he was also inexpensive to employ. During his stay in Bristol, Brunel had passed his time by completing his entry for the contest to find an engineer for the proposed Clifton bridge, and he was looking for clients. His solution to

Flags and funnels.

the silting problem was characteristically simple. 'The water is stagnant', he said, 'Just keep it moving'—and off he went to design a system of flaps at Netham Weir and culverts downstream. The latter course was adopted and the first scraper dredger built.

Brunel remained the port's consultant engineer for twenty years. He was the last of the old style 'free-lance' engineers, for the appointment of permanent staff engineers followed. He was not consulted often. This was not likely to have worried him for at this time he was busy with the 'Great Western Railway' from London to Bristol and the construction of the three ships that were his legacy to naval architecture.

The origins of the passenger-carrying ocean steamship can be traced to Bristol, directly from the completion of the Bristol–London railway line. Brunel had emerged as an engineer of importance with acceptance of his design for the Clifton Suspension Bridge and in 1833 he was appointed as engineer to the Great Western Railway. The story of the railways in Bristol is too well known to need repetition here, but at a GWR board meeting in 1835, Brunel argued for carrying the service on to New York by steamship. His ideas did not impress some of the directors, but Thomas Guppy backed the idea and the Great Western Steamship Company was formed. William Patterson laid the keel of the world's first ocean liner at his Bristol yard and the *Great Western* entered the water of the Floating Harbour on July 19th, 1837. The ship went round to the Thames under sail to have engines fitted and returned to Bristol in April 1838. As she lay in Kingroad loading for her maiden voyage, the 1,340 ton *Great Western* had cost her owners £65,000. Now came news of a rival as Liverpool owners chartered a small Irish coasting steamer called *Sirius* in an attempt to beat the Bristol ship across. In the event, *Sirius* started from Cork three days before the *Great Western* left Kingroad on April 8th, 1838, yet she entered New York harbour only six hours ahead of the Bristol steamer! The *Great Western's* passage had taken only fourteen days and her owners immediately announced a regular trans-atlantic service. In her first eighteen months, she made seventy crossings and carried 5,774 passengers. Trouble was experienced with the Dock Company, of course, who levied dues even though the ship never again came up to the port, but loaded in Kingroad. Ideas were mooted by Brunel to improve the dock facilities or even to build an ocean passenger terminal at Portishead, but the Dock Company would not hear of it. In 1841 an Act was obtained to build a pier at Portishead, but again the proposal fell through.

The Granary on Welsh Back survives today as a Jazz Club. It is typical of nineteenth century dock architecture.

So we turn to the building of Bristol's most famous ship and the commissioning of her worst commercial error. In 1838, the British Government issued a tender document for the lucrative American mail contract. While Samuel Cunard and his partners offered a fortnightly all-the-year round service from Liverpool with four small paddle steamers, all exactly the *Great Western's* size and speed, the Bristol based company allowed Brunel to persuade them to construct a single ship only, twice the size, built of iron (of all things!) paddle driven and sailing only in summer. Cunard got the contract, while Brunel changed his design to screw propulsion following the visit of the small screw steamer *Archimedes* to Bristol in May 1840, when Brunel was impressed by the new form of propulsion. The new ship was to be the largest in the world and William Patterson was again called in to build her in the somewhat unfamiliar material. She was so big that a new dock was built at West Wapping out of which she was floated on July 19th, 1843 in the presence of Prince Albert and 30,000 cheering Bristolians. The design was full of innovation—balanced rudder, screw drive, double bottom, metal construction, watertight bulkheads—all became standard ship construction practice.

With her engines fitted, the *Great Britain,* as the new monster was named, was unable to get out through the Cumberland Basin entrance. The Docks Company had not taken their promised action to widen the locks and the ship was only got through on a spring tide on December 12th, 1844 after the coping stones on the lock had been torn away. She sailed away from Bristol to be in turn a passenger ship, a wreck in Ireland, a troopship, and an Australia migrant carrier, and finally, her engine taken out, to become a nitrate carrier from Chile. In 1886 she had a rough time rounding the Horn and returned to the Falkland Islands where she was written off and used as a floating warehouse until 1937, when she was towed to Sparrow Cove and abandoned. She had, in the meantime, bankrupted several sets of owners.

The Cunard service from Liverpool was awarded the mail contract and was profitable and safe from its very first voyage. The Cunard Line was the result and Liverpool became Britain's largest passenger port. Bristol had missed her chance and was never to get another one. If only Brunel had built three more *Great Westerns*!

While Brunel was scheming his railways and ships, the Municipal Corporations Act of 1835 paved the way for change in Bristol. Already the formation of the Chamber of Commerce in 1822 had built up pressure for a reduction in dues at the port, and the Society also began to apply persuasion on the Council. In 1824, a request from the Chamber met with stony hostility. There was a bitter parliamentary battle in 1825 to get dues down, with some success by the Chamber. The reform of the City Council in 1835 meant that it was now elected by the people of the city, although the franchise was limited, and the old self-appointed body was gone forever. The new councillors began a campaign against the methods of the Docks Company. The Company in the meanwhile had bestirred themselves and asked Brunel in 1844 to prepare a scheme to rebuild the south entrance lock at Cumberland Basin. Still known as Brunel's lock, it was improved to 262 feet and a minimum width of fifty-four feet. The

The headquarters building of the P.B.A. in Queen Square, Bristol. Built in 1889 on the site of Woodes Rogers' house at No. 19, it was phased out in 1973 when the port H.Q. moved to Avonmouth.

—FRANK SHIPSIDES—1981—

work was the last that Brunel would perform for the city of Bristol and true to his style, he made the lock gates the first of the single leaf pattern to be designed in the United Kingdom.

In 1845, there was renewed agitation in the city for the Council to buy out the Dock Company. Various offers were turned down by the board of the company, although the financial difficulties remained and a dreadful list of dues faced the shipowner—to the Town he paid Mayor's, Water Bailiff's, Quay Warden's and Corn Measurer's fees; to the Society of Merchant Venturers wharfage, tonnage, carriage, cannage, cranage and plankage; to the Dock Company entry dues and Feeder Canal tolls. All this was driving business away and the central areas of the city declined as merchants moved and houses and factories emptied. Void rates was costing the Council £10,000 per annum. Meanwhile, the average dividend paid by the Dock Company over forty years was 1¼ per cent per annum.

The break-through came following the formation of the Free Port Association in 1846. This started an agitation that gained support from all parts of Bristol and was the prototype of that kind of body that Bristolians so much resort to in order to impress their views on the City Council. This is not to say that such bodies represent public opinion. Quite often, the reverse is true. Moreover, the citizen is often expected to support the ideas promoted with an increase in rates, and this was the very source of funds that the Association demanded should be used to buy out the Dock Company. In 1848, it succeeded in its aims and the docks were transferred to civic ownership on July 30th, 1848, following the passage in Parliament of yet another Bristol Dock Act. The Docks Committee of the City Council took over the running of the port, appointing a General manager to act for it, and Mr. R. Poole King became the first Chairman. The same system persists to this day. It has operated with success and is only now being questioned as, once more, financial problems caused a radical rethink of port administration. A rate in aid of the port of £5,650 per annum was raised in the first year and only for thirty years in the mid-twentieth century has this support not been required from the ratepayers of Bristol. It peaked at £154,000 in 1910 and was nil for the first time in 1940. The first act of the new owners was to rationalise port dues, reduce them and put Bristol back into competition with other ports on a basis from which she could stand a chance of success.

The argument about the rate in aid has raged in Bristol ever since 1848 in various degrees of turbulence, depending on dock proposals currently being considered. No sooner had the City taken over than the old question of the increase in the size of ships once again raised a threat to Bristol's position as a port. No one had done more to build or inspire others to build large ships than Brunel and now the monsters that he so clearly foresaw were becoming commonplace on the oceans. As early as 1858, schemes for the complete 'Dockisation', as the current in-word was, of the entire reach of the Avon to its mouth were being proposed. The arguments raged to and fro, with the pro-shipping lobby largely led by members of the Society, and the anti-dock view promoted by those who felt the ratepayers should be asked to pay no more. A company was formed to develop docks at Avonmouth and it is interesting to note that Councillors who opposed this idea were quite often defeated at the next elections as they came around. Powers were obtained for the Avonmouth Dock in 1864 but it was not ready to open until 1877. Another company obtained powers to build a dock at Portishead and this opened in 1879. Both the new docks at the entry to the Avon were connected to Bristol by railway. The new docks at the rivermouth immediately challenged the old city port for hegemony in the grain trade (soon to be an Avonmouth staple) and this at a time when a grain merchant, the formidable Alderman Proctor Baker, was Chairman of the Docks Committee. This time there was no delay, or lack of decision, and the City Council acquired both Avonmouth and Portishead Docks on September 1st, 1882.

Meanwhile, the port had begun to win back its prosperity. Trade boomed and with the return of good times, the shipping companies of Bristol expanded in all their native and often idiosyncratic glory. Mark Whitwill's Great Western Steamship Line re-opened passenger services to New York from Bristol with the *Arragon,* an iron screw steamer of 1,317 tons, in July, 1871. Both the *Arragon* and her successor, a second *Great Western,* were wrecked, but the company built up to a sizeable fleet all named after West Country counties—*Gloucester, Bristol, Somerset, Cornwall, Devon*—until the line closed through financial trouble in 1895. By the century's end, such famous names as Canadian Pacific, the Dominion Line, the Allan Line, Elder Dempster and others traded out of Bristol. A bevy of small companies flourished in the city docks, or were

St. Augustine's Reach in 1920.

visitors. All are now extinct or no longer come to Bristol but such names as Osborn and Wallis, Sloan's, Bratt, Brovig, Coast Lines, are a few from the litany of forgotten names of the port's past. Who now remembers Daniels' 'duff and doughboys', or even Alf Duggan's Ald Shipping Company with his ships such as *Brockley Combe*? Yet to gaze down the harbour in these years from Redcliffe Parade or some such vantage point, was to see a forest of masts and the colourful house-flags and funnels as the ships of Bristol went about their lawful occasions.

Two trades that flourished in the late nineteenth and early twentieth centuries had become especially Bristol's own—tobacco and bananas. Tobacco had been coming into Bristol for centuries. In 1660 it was accounting for a third of the city's trade, but the development of W.D. & H.O. Wills' early business into the giant Imperial Tobacco Company turned a trade into a basic industry and the vast blocks of the tobacco bonds became a familiar part of the Bristol skyline. On the other hand, bananas did not enter Avonmouth until 1900 but then Elder Dempster established their West Indian trade there and the long association with the sunny isles of the Carribean through Elders and Fyffes began. The white hulls of the banana boats were a familiar sight at the port.

As if to celebrate its returned importance, the Docks Committee built a new headquarters building at No. 19 Queen Square, which opened in 1889 and was in use until the P.B.A. moved to Avonmouth in 1973.

Even the new port at Avonmouth soon proved too small for Bristol's expanding trade. After the usual arguments about dockisation or dock construction and trade versus ratepayer, a scheme was proposed in October, 1900 for a larger dock at Avonmouth with Barry and Baker as principal engineers. Objectors called for a town poll and the new works were approved by 25,251 to 9,377 votes.

The works were inaugurated by the Prince of Wales (later George V) on March 5th, 1902 and the Prince announced that they would be called the Royal Edward Dock after his father Edward VII. The new dock was to be entered through a lock that would take the largest ships existing (it was enlarged when Cunard's announced the *Mauretania*) and there was also to be a large graving dock. The contract was complete by July 9th, 1908 when the genial King Edward and Queen Alexandra sailed into the Royal Edward entrance in *H.M.Y. Victoria & Albert* to open the new addition to Bristol's port. The scheme was an unqualified success and Bristol was again established as a major port of the British Empire. Six years later, when war broke out in Europe, Bristol was in a position that many envied. True, she had seen the emergence of port troubles and strikes as first Ben Tillett and then Ernest Bevin led trade union demands for reasonable pay and conditions. These could be difficult as tempers rose but were usually settled fairly and the port had a good labour relations record. A transatlantic passenger service operated once again, this time by the Canadian Northern Railway to the Saint Lawrence, with the liners *Royal Edward* and *Royal George*. These were probably the best years of the twentieth century for the port of Bristol and the war could only have raised doubts about the future.

'Then all Somerset was round me and I saw the clippers ride,
High above the moonlit houses, triple-masted on the tide.
By the tall embattled church towers of the Bristol waterside.'

John Betjeman—*Bristol*

The Augusta *in the Avon.*

The Tall Ships of Avon

THE ORIGINS of the phrase 'shipshape and Bristol fashion' lie buried somewhere in the city's past when it was the major west coast port of Britain and when all its shipping was maintained in the neat and seamanlike condition that the phrase has come to mean in everyday English usage. The maritime history of the city is in part the continuing story of Bristol ships and ships have been built here for centuries. It is not stretching reason too far to argue that the city must have had shipyards almost as soon as it was first developed but we have to wait until the thirteenth century for proof of the kind that is acceptable to the historian. In November 1294, the council of Edward I ordered all the major English ports to provide a fleet of twenty galleys to strengthen the Royal squadrons in the wars with France. Bristol is on record as being one of the ports so ordered but we know little of the ships.

There is little more on the record until the late fourteenth century but as the diversion of the Frome took place in between 1240 and 1247, it is reasonable to assume that small mud docks from which the sea could be excluded at low tide by timber baulks, could have been dug along its banks. This would have taken place outside the city wall, and breached the sea wall built along the Marsh to keep the highest tides at bay. The *Great Red Book of Bristol* states that in 1475–6, when William Bird was mayor, an

Act of Parliament was passed to make any person who wished to 'break any ground in and about Bristol' for shipbuilding to first acquire a licence.

Records of Bristol-built ships become more numerous in the fifteenth century but are tantalisingly scarce about the *Mathew* in which the Cabots sailed to the New World and which vies with Brunel's steamships for the title of Bristol's most famous ship. The construction of the *Mathew* has been the subject of debate amongst naval archictects, and historians even differ in the spelling of the ship's name. The late Charles MacInnes sticks boldly to *Matthew* in his *Bristol: A Gateway of Empire* while others use the more medieval form. The most we can say of the *Mathew* is that she was probably little more than one hundred feet in length, if that, and of about eighty tons burden. That she was decked in is almost certain, and she was probably new, though we are ignorant about how and where she was constructed. Yet her name stands in history along with those of the *Santa Maria,* flagship of Christopher Columbus (and another mystery ship) and the *Mayflower* that carried the Pilgrims to New England. All three played their parts in transplanting the seeds of European thought on the American continent and the eventual flowering of new conceptions of human freedom and dignity.

The name of *Mathew* appears in the records of the Bristol customs for several years after the Cabots' 1497 voyage and shipbuilding activity is on record throughout the sixteenth century. In these years the granting of bounties by the Lord High Admiral to encourage ship construction became a general practice and Bristol shipowners took ample advantage of the arrangements. So we find names such as *Mary Redclyf* and *Golden Lion* beginning to appear in contemporary records. In his *Bristol Privateers and Ships of War,* published in 1930, Powell puts forward the suggestion that the *Golden Lion* of 1574 was the largest English trader of the day. She may well have been at 600 tons but there is nothing to prove that she was built at Bristol. Another civic record mentions the ship *Minion* of Bristol in 1581. This ship, together with the *Great Unicorn, Handmaid* and *Aid* are in Bristol records as having taken part in the operations against the Spanish Armada in 1588. The *Minion* has the battle honour 'Armada' but little else is known. Certainly both Sir Francis Drake and Sir Walter Raleigh visited the Bristol area in the Armada years to investigate the supply of oak for the Royal shipyards. The Forest of Dean became a major national source of both timber and iron and much of its annual production went down river to Bristol. The supply of oak greatly concerned the ministers of James I and that monarch set up a survey of the Royal forests. This was done in 1610 when the annual felling was running at 80,000 trunks. James discovered that the forest stock was only 350,000 throughout the country, of which only half were suitable for shipbuilding. Orders went out immediately for massive acorn planting, something to be expected of a nation which firmly believed that the Spanish Armada had sailed with orders that 'they should yet be sure not to leave a tree standing in the Forest of Dean'.

Half a century later, we find that great servant of admiralty, Samuel Pepys, concerned with the same subject of naval timber. 'Up by four or five o'clock, and to the office' he wrote on June 20th, 1661, 'and there drew up the agreement between the King and Sir John Winter about the Forrest of Deane'. Seven years later, Pepys got an Act passed to plant and enclose 11,000 acres of derelict land in Dean. From this act of foresight came many of Nelson's first rates and the eventual safety of Britain in Napoleonic times. Pepys' term of office at the Admiralty was distinguished not least by his insistence on accurate records and we have a full list of the warships built in Bristol during the seventeenth century for the Royal and Commonwealth Navies. Largest of these was the *Edgar* sixty-four guns of 1669 and the *Northumberland* seventy guns of 1679. Samuel Pepys came down to Bristol himself to inspect progress on the *Edgar*. In the diary for June 13th, 1688, he writes 'walked with my wife and people through the city, which in every respect another London, that one can hardly know it . . . leaving my wife . . . I to see the quay, which is a most large and noble place; and to see the new ship building by Bally, neither he nor Furzer being in town. It will be a fine ship. Spoke with the foreman, and did give the boys who kept the cabin 2s.' It was on this day that Mr. Pepys dined with Mr. Butts and enjoyed 'plenty of brave wine and above all Bristol Milk'.

The *Edgar* collected a crop of battle honours—Solebay 1672, Texel 1673, Beachy Head 1693 and was at Barfleur in May, 1692 when a combined Anglo-Dutch fleet under Russell defeated the French squadrons of de Tourville and finally secured the Protestant succession under William III. Other Bristol-built ships by Bailey at Barfleur were the *Oxford* fifty-four guns of 1674 and the *Northumberland.* The latter was subsequently lost in the great gale of 1703.

As the seventeenth century passed, so the city expanded outside the old walls, the old Marsh was enclosed by quays and the elegant Queen's Square spread itself across the area, including the new Custom House of 1709. Hence the shipyards were forced to find new sites lower down the Avon, and the Marsh was left behind together with such wet docks as Gib Tayler, located where today stands the Bush warehouse.

Some builders used the Limekiln Dock, a creek at the foot of Brandon Hill which was made into a drydock in the late eighteenth century and used as late as 1903. Nicholas Blannin built ships at Redcliff Backs from 1747 to 1839 and a number of small yards thrived along St. Augustine's Reach western bank—Teast's, Manfield, Tippetts and Peters—at various times up until 1885 when the Albert Dock and the Mud Dock were filled in by the City Council for quay improvements.

It was near the Merchants Dock at Hotwells, begun as Champion's in 1762 and bought by the Society in 1772, that the next significant name in Bristol shipbuilding occurs. Here James Martin Hilhouse, son of a wealthy Bristol family whose fortunes had been founded in shipowning

H.M.S. Arethusa, *the famous frigate built in Bristol in 1781.*

and privateering, turned his back on those adventurous and risky investments and set up a shipyard. In doing so he set in motion an enterprise that was to endure for just over two centuries and provide Bristol with some of her most famous ships. The first was probably the *Exeter* of 730 tons launched in 1773, and delivered to the West India Company. A heavy demand for fighting ships during the rebellion of the American colonists in 1775 and the subsequent war with France, led to Hilhouse obtaining his first Admiralty order in 1778 for the frigate *Medea* and this was followed in succession by *Crescent* 1779, *Termagent* 1780, *Arethusa* and *Diomede* 1781, *Serapis* 1782, *Trusty* 1782, *Nassau* and *Melampus* 1785. To produce all these warships and other orders, Hilhouse opened another yard across the river on a site just north of the Ashton railway swing bridge of today, but closed it when the war ended.

All these Bristol frigates were in action at some time in their careers. *Medea* fought under Rodney in North America and was in Hughes' Indian fleet against Suffren. *Diomede* was wrecked in 1795 but *Serapis* served until 1826 and should not be confused with the *Serapis* of 1779 which surrendered to John Paul Jones that same year. *Nassau* was the largest ship built in Bristol at the time and was almost large enough (sixty-four guns) to lie in the line-of-battle. *Melampus* was present at Sir John Borlase Warren's defeat of a French squadron off the Donegal coast on October 12th, 1797, when, under the command of Captain Graham Moore, R.N., she forced the surrender of the French frigate *Coquille*.

Whether the H.M.S. *Arethusa* launched in Bristol by Hilhouse on August 23rd, 1779 is the *'Saucy Arethusa'* of Prince Hoare's famous song is questionable. The song describes the action with the French frigate *Belle Poule* in June 1775 and the *Arethusa* engaged that day could only have been the prize *Arethuse* taken in 1759. Yet many authorities give the nickname to the Bristol-built frigate, including the Admiralty records. The Bristol ship acquired a long list of battle honours that outdid her predecessor—Warren's frigate action of 1794, the capture of the Spanish frigate *Pomona* in 1806 and the taking of Curacao in 1807—she was in action at them all. Her tonnage was 948, she measured 141 × 39 feet and carried twenty-eight eighteen pounders, ten nine pounders and eight carronades. Her complement was 280. *Arethusa* was decommissioned after Napoleon's banishment to Elba in 1814 and broken up at Sheerness.

'Dockisation' from 1804 to 1809 produced problems for shipyards in Bristol and the use of the Limekiln Dock as a drydock had to cease altogether. Hilhouse got £4,238 compensation under the Dock Act in 1810, and later rebuilt the dock. It was in 1810 also that a young man named Charles Hill joined the firm and so impressed his employers that they made him a partner, soon after their important move to the south bank of the Floating Harbour in 1820. This new dockyard would be named Albion in 1848. James Martin Hilhouse died in 1822, but his sons carried on the business, taking Charles Hill into partnership in 1825. In 1845, George Hilhouse passed the business over to his partner as there were no Hilhouse sons to continue the line and the famous Bristol company of Charles Hill & Sons came into being. As shipbuilders and shipowners of the Bristol City Line, the family have played a not inconsiderable part in the history of Bristol and the last ship to be built in Albion Dockyard was sent to sea in 1977.

Before we follow the fortunes of the Bristol ships that came from Albion Dockyard, there are two other yards that we must consider among the sixty or so concerns that have built or repaired ships in Bristol in the course of the last two and a half centuries. Many of these were substantial businesses like Stothert (1844–c. 1920), Wapping Dock Company (1856–97) and the tug-builders and owners Paynes (1859–1924). But the shipyard operated by the Teast family at Wapping East on the site of present-day Bathurst Basin from 1750 to 1841 unwittingly provided the Royal Navy with the stage for its most notorious mutiny. There were four successive heads of the Teast family all named Sydenham and in 1782 the second patriarch launched a thirty-two gun frigate of 716 tons for the Royal Navy. Their Lordships called her *Hermione* and in 1797, the year of the fleet mutinies at the Nore and Spithead, she was the scene of one of the most murderous uprisings ever to have taken place on the high seas. There is little doubt that the crew were provoked into action by the tyrannical behaviour of their commander, Captain Hugh Pigot. Pigot used the lash unsparingly and was accustomed to flog the last man down from aloft after a change of sail. He had a bad reputation in the fleet and his crew were probably a rough lot to begin with, as such an officer would not attract good seamen to his ship. *Hermione* was taking in top-sails off the Porto Rican coast when Pigot threatened to flog the last man off the mizzen top-

The barque Favell, *last tall ship to be built in Bristol.*

sail yard. In the ensuing rush, two seamen fell to the quarter deck and were killed. Pigot's only comment was reported to have been 'throw the lubbers overboard'. The following day the crew mutinied, slew Pigot and all his officers and took the ship into the Spanish Mainland port of La Guayra, where *Hermione* became part of the Armada Real.

The *Hermione* was recaptured in October 1799 in a thrilling cutting-out action by the ship's boats of H.M.S. *Surprise* under Captain Sir Edward Hamilton, who entered the harbour of Porto Gabello in the small hours of October 25th. Hamilton had to pass under 200 guns on his way in, and his crew actually had the *Hermione* underway before the main force of the Spanish crew had been overcome on the main deck.

The other Bristol shipyard that gained its place in British maritime history is that of William Patterson (1795–1869) the orphan boy from Arbroath who became a London shipwright's apprentice and in 1830 set up his shipyard in Bristol, having first worked for Scott at his Wapping East yard and been married in St. Mary Redcliffe in 1823. Patterson was by far the most versatile of the Bristol shipwrights and the story of his famous partnership with Brunel has been told elsewhere in these pages. In the next thirty-nine years, he was to be responsible for something like sixty vessels of all sizes from small yachts like his own *Adiante* to the largest ships in the world like the *Great Britain* and the unfortunate *Demerara* whose wreck in the Avon in 1861 almost bankrupted Patterson. Nevertheless, she became the world's largest sailing ship as the *British Empire* and we shall meet her again in Chapter 8.

Warships were again on the list of Bristol order books in the 1850s when both Hills and Patterson built gunboats for the Navy. Hills had built covered yards at Albion Dockyard and celebrated the firm's first warship order for fifty years by hiring a brass band for the launch. The large crowd that gathered to watch the ceremony on March 3rd, 1856 were later said to be disappointed by the diminutive appearance of the 233 ton H.M.S. *Hardy*. Patterson lost money on his part of the contract and had to sell off his Wapping yard to pay his creditors. But he continued in business in the Great Western Dock and in his later years produced some of the great fast square riggers whose beautiful hull lines he had foreshadowed in his little racing yachts of years before. In 1865 Patterson started work on four fully rigged ships and two of these, the *Royal Adelaide* and the *Royal Sovereign,* both of 1,385 tons, were the largest iron sailing vessels built at Bristol. They were true representatives of the great days of the tall ships which were to carry on economic trading for nearly threequarters of a century after the coming of steam, which would eventually drive them from the sea lanes. William Patterson retired to Liverpool in 1865 and died in 1869.

This left the Albion Dockyard of Charles Hill & Sons as the premier Bristol shipyard. As early as 1813 the firm built Bristol's first steamships, the *Charlotte* and the *Hope,* as river tugs and later in 1823 the city's first seagoing steamers, the *George IV* and the *Palmerston*. These were for the War Office Steam Packet Company to carry mail and passengers on the 200 mile passage to Cork. This was a private concern despite its title and it was to carry on in the trade to Ireland and expand it to continental ports through several changes of title until it became the Bristol Steam

The Wells City *of the Bristol City Line was typical of small traders built at Albion Dockyard in the early years of the century. This was the second vessel of the name, built by Hills in 1890 and the first built for their own line.*

Navigation Company in 1877. Nevertheless, steam came to Bristol more slowly than elsewhere. In this same year of 1877, of every five vessels towed up to Bristol by Kings' tugs, four were sailing ships. Steam would triumph in the long run, that was evident, and several Bristol owners realised the inevitable. In 1869 Mark Whitwill had set up his emigrant steamer line to New York, although U.S. immigration quotas forced him to change over to cargo ships in the '80s. He resurrected the Great Western Steamship Company's name and his *Arragon* and *Great Western* traded successfully for a number of years. Then in 1879, Charles Hill, son of the founder of the family, formed the Bristol City Line and Albion Dockyard was to build five of its steamships in the next four decades—*Wells City* 1890, *Bristol City* 1899, *Boston City* 1917, *New York City* 1917, *Bristol City*

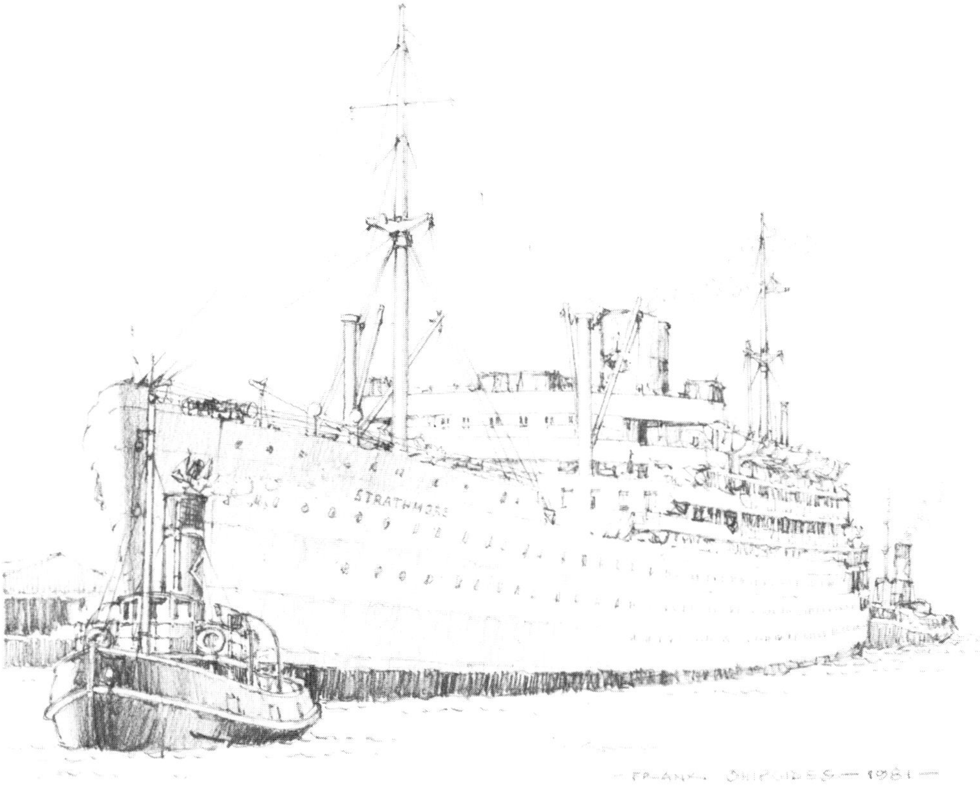

A visiting P. & O. liner, the Strathmore, *at Avonmouth in 1937. Cruise ships still call occasionally.*

(3) 1919, *Boston City* (3) 1920. The firm already owned a considerable fleet of sailing vessels but it now began to sell these and the yard was building almost exclusively steamships as the '90s started. Even so, Hills built a final series of five steel barques ending with the *Favell* of 1895, named after a lady of the family, Miss Favell Hill who performed the launching ceremony. *Favell* was Bristol's last tall ship built in the city. Hill's eventually sold her to Finnish owners who ran her in the Australian grain trade until 1934.

So the tall ships passed but Bristol would go on building ships in the new century and to each of their products Charles Hill & Sons added a company ornamental plaque with the firm's name, and engraving of Brunel's Suspension Bridge and the legend 'Shipshape and Bristol

Fashion'. It was placed on the largest ship ever built in Bristol, the Spanish steamer *Neptune,* 3,554 tons and 325 feet long, launched in 1921 and later named *Artea Mendi*. Finally it was placed on the last ship built at Albion Dockyard, the *Miranda Guinness* of 1976.

Finally, in this tale of Bristol shipbuilders and Bristol ships, let us recall those ships of the Royal Navy that have carried the name of the city, and also some of the naval vessels that have served here. In all the fleet has used the name seven times for fighting vessels and they have between them been awarded twelve battle honours. The first H.M.S. *Bristol* was built in 1653 by the Commonwealth and therefore started life as anything but a king's ship. It is thought that the name was used to commemorate the Parliamentary seige of the city in 1645, but neither Charles II or Prince Rupert (who had good cause) saw fit to change the name at the Restoration. The ship was built at Portsmouth, carried forty-eight guns and first saw action in the Mediterranean in 1658 against Spanish pirates. She was at the Four Days Battle in 1666, when the Dutch trounced Admiral Myngs, who lost his life as did *Bristol's* captain Philomel Bacon. Other actions followed at Orfordness 1666 and Solebay 1672 and the Texel 1673, but this ship is better known for the diary kept by her chaplain, the Rev. Henry Teonge, which has become a much-quoted source of seventeenth century naval lore.

Bristol was rebuilt in 1683, later serving in the West Indies and a gruesome scene took place on her quarter deck at Plymouth on April 16th, 1707 when Captains Wade and Kirkby were executed for cowardice, disobedience to orders and neglect of duties. They had deserted Admiral Benbow in action against the French in the West Indies. This long-lived ship met her end in the English Channel on April 25th, 1709 when she sank after battle damage by the French.

The second *Bristol* was built in 1711 and served under Vernon and later Anson at Finisterre in 1747. She was broken up in 1768 and replaced in 1775 by the third *Bristol*. She was Sir Peter Parker's flagship at Charleston in June 1776 and lost her commander Captain Morris and forty of the crew. During these years in the West Indies, one of her officers was a certain Lt. Horatio Nelson. On June 20th, 1783, this *Bristol* was in Hughes' defeat at Cuddalore by the brilliant French strategist Suffren, although both Admirals were unaware that peace had been signed five months

The launch of the Miranda Guinness *in July 1976, the last commercial vessel to be built in the City Docks.*

earlier! The third *Bristol* was broken up in 1801 and in 1809 the battleship *Agincourt* was renamed *Bristol* until her sale in 1814. The fifth holder of the name was a screw frigate of 1861, built at Woolwich and used for a time as a cadets' training ship until 1883 when she was sold out of the service.

The sixth *Bristol* was the famous light cruiser of 1910, built on the Clyde and whose wartime adventures we shall relate in Chapter 10. Finally there is the splendid present day holder of the name, the Type 82 destroyer built on the Tyne and commissioned at Avonmouth on March 31st, 1973, a nice compliment to the city by the Navy and a unique occasion. The ship, by far the largest to carry the name, has been a regular visitor to the city and carries the honorary freedom, the highest civic honour.

No book on Royal Navy links with Bristol would be complete without mention of the R.N.V.R. drillships which have served the Severn Division of that distinguished service over the years. First there was the frigate *Daedalus* of 1826 which burst into the newspapers of credulous Victorians in August 1848 when her crew claimed to have shadowed a sea-serpent in the South Atlantic. The *Illustrated London News* solemnly informed its readers that 'this must be the most authentic record of the animal in modern times'. The *Daedalus* served at Mardyke for fifty years from 1861 to 1911 when she was broken up. Her successor was the sloop *Flying Fox,* named after the Derby winner of 1890, and possibly one of the ugliest warships ever to come from the drafting board of a naval architect. Yet generations of Bristol naval volunteers loved her and she served them well from 1923 to 1973. The City Docks lost something of their attractiveness with her passing, the old ship being towed away on Sunday, March 18th, 1973.

They've all gone now, those brave three-masters of Bristol's past. The Avon is as near peace as the relentless tide will allow and the Floating Harbour is given over to the sand suckers, the yachtsman and the wind surfer. To any of the older generation who knew the city docks of yore, when Redcliffe spire rose above a forest of masts, or to those lucky enough to have attended a launch at Albion Dockyard, Robert Southey took on the role of a latter-day prophet when he sat down in his house at Westbury-on-Trym in 1799 and wrote:

> 'Avon! I gaze and know
> The lesson emblem'd in thy varying way;
> It speaks of human joys that rise so slow,
> So rapidly decay.'

'As to the seat of the city and its environs it surpasses all I ever saw. A great commercial city in the midst of cornfields, meadows and woods, and the ships, coming into the centre of it miles from anything like sea . . .'

William Cobbett—*Rural Rides 1830*

The sand-boat Bowline *passing Pill ferry.*

Life on the River

LIKE HER great rival London, the city of Bristol stands at the head of a tidal river, inland from the sea. As we have seen, the city grew up around an easy crossing point, protected on the east by Bristol Castle, and on the west by the cliffs of the Avon Gorge.

As the city's trade prospered, so the river became its lifeline, an umbilical cord through which the lifeblood of prosperity flowed, as the ships came and went. In all this activity, the river developed a life of its own, raising small communities on its banks, creating craft for its own special purposes and giving a peculiar Bristol Avon character to the trows, hobbles, skiffs, tugs and pleasure steamers which used its waters.

For the Bristolian, the river proper starts at Hotwells, at the entrance to Cumberland Basin. Everything upstream is merely 'the Docks' or, if you are a Bristolian who think yourself a little 'up market', you may even say 'the floating harbour'. This curious compartmenting of the city probably comes down from the days when Bristol was cooped up within the old city walls—a state of affairs that lasted until almost the end of the eighteenth century. Even the old Bristol Bridge was said to 'cross the haven' and retained its shops and houses until 1768.

Although there had been development outside the walls in the reign of Anne when Queen Square appeared, it was not until the turn of the eighteenth century that Bristol really began to expand. Then the prosperous merchants turned to the cliffs above the river entrance, in order to surpass their neighbours in fashionable Bath, and create a series of Georgian crescents that swept along the north wall of the Avon Gorge—Windsor Terrace, The Paragon, Cornwallis Crescent, Royal York Crescent—names for the age that turned Clifton into the showplace suburb of England.

The riches of Bristol created Clifton above the river and the famous came to wonder—and stay awhile. Macaulay lived in Caledonia Place. Southey visited friends from his home across the Downs, and the tiny Princess Victoria toddled down the Zig Zag. Years later, the Queen would discover that her dear friend, the Empress Eugénie, spent part of her school days in Royal York Crescent.

Today, Clifton retains its gentle aristocratic atmosphere despite all the pressures of modern city life, and its residents are wont to show a robust and healthy opposition to any developer who seeks to change the scene. Below, on the river bank, Hotwells has suffered the full impact of the twentieth century, but even the curving arches of the Cumberland Basin scheme are broken almost every tide, as the elegant Plimsoll Bridge swings the road aside to allow sand boats to pass into the river.

These sand boats, or technically sand suckers, are the backbone of the building industry, and a small fleet of them has worked out of the City Docks for years. Small and often battered in appearance, they look what they are—working boats that ply every day of the year in all weathers to suck pure sand from the bed of the channel off Flatholm or to work the gravel deposits. They return with cargoes that form neat cones on the quayside until hauled away to form the core of new buildings. The old local sand dredging companies gave their boats evocative west country and Bristol names—*Steepholm, Portway, Camerton, Dunkerton* were but a few—but even they are now merging into groups and the old names are disappearing. One famous name at least remains. The *Harry Brown* is named after the late Mr. Harry Brown, who developed the family lighterage, towage and salvage interests into one of the city's prominent businesses, the Holms Sand and Gravel Company. Harry Brown was a real Bristol 'character'. He had eleven sons, one of whom, Sir Kenneth Brown, became Lord Mayor of Bristol and Master of the Society of Merchant Venturers.

The same years that saw the development of Clifton were those when the first steam boats appeared on the river. Here was an invention in which Bristol could take real interest. Until now, ships coming up the river, whilst getting some help from the incoming tide, usually relied on boats or the patient drag horses that plodded along the towpath. The first practical use of steam power in ships in use in Bristol was for towage, and tugs have been part of the harbour scene ever since.

The Badminton*, a sandsucker of Bristol Sand & Gravel Company, familiar sight on the Bristol Avon.*

The early steam boats, built with traditional wooden hulls, and some auxiliary sail, usually had their engines amidships, driving paddlewheels on either beam. The paddle-boxes took up a third or so of the overall length, giving the little vessels a powerful appearance. It was the engines themselves that caused problems. Usually of single cyclinder pattern, they had available only about 15 p.s.i. of steam. Hence, the cylinders were large and the piston rod had an irritating habit of stopping at top dead centre when operating at slow speed. As this was usually when the ship was approaching a berth or quay, pandemonium reigned in the engine room while the engineers and firemen pulled the recalcitrant crank over by using hooked rods. Later, twin cylinder or compound diagonal designs overcame this problem, to the great relief of skippers, who could only wait topsides while their charge drove on, out of control, and into the quayside (unless the engineers were smart!). Capricious as these engines were, they were reliability itself when compared to the boilers that supplied the steam. Accurate measurement of boiler pressure was something of a hit-and-miss business in the early days. There were no accepted safety limits (these would come later with I. K. Brunel) and engineers would often tie down safety valves in the search for more speed. Sometimes their judgment failed, and there are several records of boiler explosions in Bristol. The most spectacular was probably that of the *Black Eagle,* a steam tug which blew up in the Avon opposite the Hotwell on November 1st, 1866. Parts of the ship sailed hundreds of feet into the air and some landed in the garden behind the 'General Draper' Inn, on the far side of Hotwells Road. Part of the boiler was found in Price's Buildings, 300 feet above the river. The crew of eight all died in the blast.

The paddle tugs, of which the *Charlotte* of 1813 was the first (and Bristol's first steamship), lasted on the channel until the end of the nineteenth century. By then, towage had been taken over by dozens of small screw tugs that hurried here and there around the harbour, making the journey up the Feeder Canal, with lighterloads of materials for the new industries in Barton Hill and Brislington, or carefully shepherding an outward-bound tramp down to Kingroad, there to await a fresh client for the return up river.

Many of the towage concerns were single-ship family businesses, and two or three have survived in family hands, even into the 1970s and 1980s. Ashmead, Browns', Head, Roberts, Paynes' are all famous names in Bristol port history.

Nearly all the smaller tugs went for scrap years ago. But the memories remain. The *Ariel* was a puffer tug used in George Head's fleet to tow his numerous barges. Head also operated the 'Penny' steamers *Emily* and *Kate* which ran from the Drawbridge to Hotwells for the single fare of one penny! Payne's *Elf,* reputedly the fastest tug on the Channel in her day, was part of a fleet that brought small sailing craft up-river to Bathurst Basin.

Of all the Bristol towage concerns, there is none more illustrious than that of C. J. King & Sons Ltd., which was founded in 1850 and is still run by members of the same family. King's tugs have always had a reputation for smart appearance and have been regularly involved in state occasions. *Sea Prince* handled the Royal Yacht *Victoria and Albert* when King Edward

VII opened the Royal Edward Dock on July 9th, 1908. Sixty-nine years later, on August 8th, 1977, King Edward's great grand-daughter Elizabeth II opened Royal Portbury Dock in H.M.Y. *Britannia,* handled by King's *Sea Merrimac.* Earlier, in July 1970, another of the famous tugs *Sea Alert* had helped the returning s.s. *Great Britain* up river to the City Docks.

King's (and Bristol's) last paddle-tug was the famous *Merrimac* (there is a *Sea Merrimac* in King's present fleet) and she provided an interesting link with another important branch of Bristol river life.

On the north bank of the Avon, just below the Hotwell, there stands the remains of the passenger landing pontoon, silent monument to the golden days of the excursion steamers. The fashionable crowds that had gathered on the riverside during the heyday of the Hotwell had departed forever, when the so-called healing waters had proved rather less therapeutic. In the 1880s, a new crowd, composed of artisans, tradespeople and middle class ladies and gents of the commercial world, arrived at Hotwells to pack the saloon paddle steamers of the two Scots brothers, Captains Peter and Alexander Campbell.

Bristolians, born in sight and sound of ships, were never adverse to trips on the river, even if their daily work had little to do with maritime affairs. Steamer excursions began to run from Bristol as early as 1817, and trips to the twin islands Flatholm and Steepholm were popular. In his history of the Bristol pleasure steamers, Grahame Farr attributes this to the taverns which traded on each island, free from excise duty and opening restrictions. Could it be that nineteenth century Bristol pioneered the 'Duty-free' excursion? Of special interest, there was an excursion on September 8th, 1838 to view the departure of the *Great Western* for New York.

Later in the century, the paddle tugs were pressed into excursion service. One of the earliest was the *Sampson,* owned by the Bristol General S.N. Company and used to handle the *Great Britain.* With careful organisation, a surprising number of people could be squeezed aboard a paddle tug, therefore, at weekends and Bank Holidays, many of the local tugs were dusted down, fitted out with deck chairs and cushions, and advertised as 'splendid excursion steamers of great comfort and safety'. Mostly the trips were down river to Avonmouth and a quick dash into the

The Samuel Plimsoll *and the* Cabot, *two of the numerous craft operated by the Port of Bristol Authority. The* Samuel Plimsoll *is a bucket dredger, one of a fleet used to clear away silt from the Port.*

upper Channel, returning on the same tide. With anything of a sea running, the progress of the tripper was inevitably damp and uncomfortable, even on the larger tugs, which ventured as far afield as Ilfracombe in the South West to Chepstow in the North. The *Merrimac* was ideal for this work, and King's ran her on pleasure trips from 1883 to 1890. By this time, the saloon paddle steamer had captured all the worthwhile trade.

Many owners have been credited by historians with running the first of the new style pleasure steamers on the Bristol Channel. As far as Bristol is concerned, the record probably belongs to the *Bonnie Doon,* a Clyde built iron paddler which appeared on public show at The Drawbridge on May 18th, 1886. The success of *Bonnie Doon* in 1886 encouraged the arrival of Peter and Alec Campbell's *Waverley* in 1887, chartered by a syndicate headed by no less a Bristol celebrity than Frank Wills.

To a society whose only prime movers were the railway locomotive and the horse, the novelty and adventure of an excursion by sea was a great attraction. The spotless white funnels of the Campbell ship, the acrid taste of steam and smoke, the clank of crank and splutter of paddle wheel churning the muddy Avon, all this must have fascinated a generation yet to see an aeroplane or listen to a wireless set!

Campbell's excursions were a success from their inception, and, in the years that followed, the brothers drove all opposition from the Bristol Channel. Edwards and Robertson, the Barry Railway Company, George Nurse, the Yellow Funnel Fleet, all fell victims to the commercial hard tactics and navigation dash of the Campbells. Racing between steamers climaxed when *Ravenswood,* with Alec Campbell in command, collided with the Welsh *Lorna Doone* off Weston-super-Mare on June 5th, 1893. Captain Campbell lost his licence for six months in the resultant enquiry, but his company went on from strength to strength.

In the years that followed, the Scots brothers launched a series of paddlers whose names have become part of Bristol's maritime history, and certainly part of the nostalgic past for the older generation who remember *Britannia* and *Westward Ho, Ravenswood* and *Cambria, Glen Avon* and *Glen Usk.* Each winter the fleet laid up at Underfall Yard, where Captain Peter presided as Engineer-in-chief and prepared his charges for next season. During this time he lived in Clifton, and eventually died in 1938 at Wotton-under-Edge, aged eighty.

The heyday of the pleasure steamers lasted from the 1890s until the Second World War. After 1945, the paddlers had to compete with the family motor car and an age that sought its pleasure elsewhere. The last of them, the *Bristol Queen,* was withdrawn in 1967. Campbells finally ceased services in 1980 and today Channel excursions are operated by a preservation society, which still brings a paddler, the *Waverley* to Bristol each year. The memories remain, the stories of *Ravenswood* and *Britannia* lose nothing in the telling and many an elderly Bristolian will recount his tale of blue skies, calm seas, gargantuan meals and lovely ships in the days when all Bristol went 'down Combe wiv Campbells!'

Brunel's masterly Clifton Suspension bridge spans the Avon Gorge at a point just below the pontoons; talked about in 1753, designed in 1830 and finally opened in December 1864. All Bristol knows that the bridge is 702 feet from pier to pier and 290 feet above the river bed. Originally, the trustees thought it would be toll free by 1944!

Below the bridge the river turns gently north until the great expanse of Sea Mills reach broadens almost to a lake at high tide and floods the tiny harbour where Roman galleys laid up nearly 2,000 years ago. Ahead is the Horseshoe Bend, dangerous to vessels of 200 foot length, and impossible for those over 300 feet. Tidal forces in the bend can be very deceptive and many a crew had cause to remember this length of the river. Below the Horseshoe Bend, the quieter waters of Hungroad formed an anchoring ground for small tide-bound vessels on their way up to Bristol. Traces of mooring points can still be seen on the rocks hereabouts, and prominent among the anchored vessels were the Severn trows, the indigenous ships of the upper Bristol Channel.

Trow is a medieval word for trough and the open hold, headed by a bluff bow and ending in a transom stern makes the likeness clear. The early trows were square rigged and traded as far up the Severn as Ironbridge, bringing cargoes down to Bristol and the Welsh ports. Trows sailed well up the Wye, but the open hold made them so vulnerable, that they rarely ventured beyond a line from Watchet in Somerset to Barry in the north.

The Severn trows appeared in many versions, a sloop rig and later that of a ketch replacing the original square sail. Normally they would be sixty-five to seventy feet long with a beam of eighteen feet maximum and drew about six feet when loaded to seventy tons. In later years, when they rarely carried more than a crew of two, trows were hard work, requiring anything from handling the elderly rig to towing the ship around bends with the boat that was always towed astern. Trows were built to last and the record is held by the *William* of Gloucester, built in 1809 and lost in 1939. The last trows went out of use in the 1930s, and the hulls of the survivors were used as lighters on this same Bristol Avon.

And so we come to Pill, whose tiny harbour and village on the south bank, about one mile from the river mouth, has for centuries been the home of the local Bristol pilots. A ferry ran for years across to Shirehampton where William III, homeward bound from Ireland and the Boyne, paused to visit his friend Sir Robert Southwell at Kingsweston House.

The maiden voyage of Brunel's paddle steamer The Great Western *in 1837.*

FRANK SHIPSIDES 1981

SHIPSIDES — 1981

Balmoral *and* Devonia, *last survivors of Campbell's fleet of pleasure steamers, laid up at Bristol in 1980.*

Although historical record does not support the claim, Bristol pilots have long proclaimed James George Ray as the first 'official' Channel pilot. He it was, so the story goes, who piloted Cabot's *Matthew* to sea in May 1497. Certainly, Pilot George Ray serviced the outward bound *Great Western* in 1837, and another Ray, this time William of the cutter *Triumph,* No. 14, saw the *Great Britain* safely on her way in 1844. The pilots of Pill cruised the Channel in their sturdy cutters, the designs for which remain classics of small ship naval architecture. Speed was essential to catch and go alongside cruising merchant vessels and offer pilotage ahead of one's rivals. Seakeeping ability in all weathers necessitated a sturdy hull.

For centuries, the sole pilotage authority on the Channel was the Society of Merchant Venturers to whom the Mayor and Corporation delegated powers in 1611. From then until 1861, Bristol was in control of even Cardiff, Newport and Gloucester, when the Bristol Channel Pilotage Act of 1861 gave those cities their own pilotage areas, and control of Bristol Pilotage returned to the City Council, where it remains to this day.

A Severn Trow passes a square-rigger in the Bristol Channel. The open hull of the trow and the canvas sides made it vulnerable to heavy seas when down channel.

Bratt boats in the City Docks.

Many of the Bristol pilots came from this village of Pill, a corruption of Crockerne, or Crewkerne Pill. There was no love lost between the people of Pill and the citizens of Bristol. The merchants of Bristol looked on the Pill men as little better than pirates or smugglers and there is no doubt that some were actively engaged in both activities. Any caught red-handed were likely to be hanged by their feet from Prince Street Bridge to await death from the rising tide! Pill, on the other hand regarded Bristol as a large neighbour seeking to suppress a small but independent community. The author has heard similar views expressed in North Somerset today!

It was during the nineteenth century that the pilot cutters of Pill developed into the superb service boats that gained their place in the history of ship design. A typical Channel pilot cutter, always known to the Pill men as a 'skiff', would be locally built by such men as the Cooper family—one man and a boy—and cost around £400 all complete! Frame and heel were of oak, with oak or elm planking and pine decking and masts. The Bristol boats were identified with their number on the mainsail. Bristol pilots were the last in Britain to cruise for trade and there was great competition to own the fastest skiff. In fine weather a pilot would board direct, but in heavy seas the skiff worked into the leaside of the ship and the pilot was rowed across in the skiff's punt. If the crew were short handed (there were seldom more than two) the pilot rowed himself and kicked the punt free at the foot of the boarding ladder! By day the cutters flew the red and white pilot flag and were supposed to burn a blue flare every fifteen minutes at night.

The tales of the pilot skiffs are many—none more typical than that of the *Emma,* which once boarded a ship of Lundy at 4.30 p.m., sailed with her up to Avonmouth, recovered her pilot and returned to Lundy by 8.00 a.m. the next morning to board an incoming Elder Dempster liner—an average of ten knots over the ground.

The era of the sailing pilots ended in 1914–18, but Pill today is still the home of some of the Bristol pilots, who deal with radar and bulk carriers, and speed out to arriving vessels in fast launches.

The Avon enters the Channel at Kingroad, the river mouth anchorage at the entrance to Avonmouth Docks. Nowhere in the kingdom will you find a stream with a more diverse history or one that has been so much an effective stimulus to the development of a city as the Avon has to Bristol.

'Our brows are bound with spindrift and the weed is on our knees;
Our loins are battered 'neath us by the swinging, smoking seas.
From reef and rock and skerry—over headland, ness and voe—
The coastwise lights of England watch the ships of England go!'

Rudyard Kipling—*The Coastwise Lights*

s.s. Gypsy *wrecked in the Avon, May 12th, 1878.*

Storm and Tempest

FROM THE earliest times, 'those who go down to sea in ships, and have their business in great waters' have prayed to their Creator in a dozen different tongues and creeds that they might go safely among the waves and return in due course to their home and family. Those left behind had no illusions about the power of the sea to destroy. 'Oh hear us when we cry to Thee,' pleaded the hymnalist, 'for those in peril on the sea.' It is no accident that the Royal National Lifeboat Institution, founded in 1824, is one of the earliest and best financed of our great national charities, or that the Trinity House of London enjoys such well earned national and international prestige.

It is one of nature's ironies that the same Providence that gave Bristol a wide highway to the world through the Severn estuary, compensated for that good fortune by making that same estuary difficult and dangerous to navigate. We have already commented on the tidal range of streams in the estuary. These have fathered the huge sandbanks that lie in wait on either side of the fairways for the unwary. To all these hazards must be added the mile upon mile of unhospitable coast which runs along the southern shore of the Bristol Channel from Cape Cornwall to Bridgwater Bay and presents few havens in its endless chain of reefs, rocks and almost vertical cliffs.

Small wonder, then, that the shores and waters, isles and points that stretch eastward from Hartland Point are marked by a numerous assortment of lights, buoys, beacons, foghorns, signal stations and lightships, all for the express purpose of providing safe guidance of the mariner bound in or out of the Bristol Channel ports.

On the major promontories of the southern shore, the Elder Brethren of Trinity House have erected great stone towers to carry the warning lights. Most of them were built in the nineteenth century, although that on Flatholm dates from 1737. That on Hartland used a fifty-nine feet high tower to raise its light 120 feet above the sea, giving visibility in good weather for twenty miles. The two Lundy lighthouses are even higher, the North and South being 165 and 175 feet respectively above the waves. Further up channel, Nash Point light on the northern shore has the highest tower of the estuary, 122 feet, although the Lynmouth Foreland displays its beams from a point 220 feet up the cliffside and is the highest in terms of altitude.

We have already referred to the lightships that used to stand watch at the Breaksea and English and Welsh grounds. The author recalls many pleasant visits to the latter with the Bristol Pilotage Committee on its annual inspection of the Western pilotage station, based at Barry. As the English and Welsh Grounds lie in comparatively sheltered waters, the Elder Brethren usually reserved one of their older vessels for the duty. The Pilotage Committee would take the opportunity to drop off a few liquid comforts (all highly unofficial conduct, of course) and would invariably be greeted by the lightship skipper—'Welcome aboard, Sir! Oldest ship in the service, Sir!' Old she may have been, but she shone as smart as any Cunarder on a maiden voyage. Bristolians have been able to see succeeding generations of lightships moored in the city. An elderly vessel that served on the E. & W. Grounds did duty in Bathurst Basin for years as the Cabot Cruising Club's H.Q. ship *John Sebastian* and a modern example is moored as a floating pub in Welsh Back at the end of King Street, across the quay from the Llandoger Trow inn. Each year, in early summer, the Port of Bristol plays host to the Elder Brethren who arrive on their annual inspection of Bristol Channel lights and buoyage in the lovely t.h.v. *Patricia*. In 1981, *Patricia,* looking as smart as ever, was in her fifth decade of service to Trinity House and due for replacement.

The prevailing winds of the Bristol Channel blow in from the West and Southwest, and some of the rollers that crash ashore on the North Devon coast have been gathering strength and speed for over two and a half thousand miles since they left the Newfoundland and Labrador Banks. In a sailing vessel, the Channel has always been an easier place to enter than to leave, and there were always casualties in gales during the sailing era. Many of these wrecks took place on Bristol's doorstep. As an example, in the great gale that swept up the estuary on the night of March 26th, 1869, dozens of vessels were driven before it. As daylight came, three ships were aground in Walton Bay near Clevedon and seven small coasters were found to have sunk either near or in Portishead. Such events were routine, and even today, when modern technology in the form of stout, powerful engines and all-seeing radar provide the seafarer with practically one hundred per cent security, accidents can and do still happen. Every year the volunteer crews of the R.N.L.I. rescue anything up to 1,000 people in operations around British coasts.

The saga—and the word is appropriate in its full sense—of the Bristol Channel lifeboats of the English shores has been told elsewhere. However, we must record here the first lifeboat station on our channel, set up in Bideford in 1824, the same year that the R.N.L.I. was founded. Stations followed at Appledore, Ilfracombe, Braunton, Morte Bay, Lynmouth, Minehead, Watchet, Burnham-on-Sea and Weston. In the early days, these stations were provided with the pulling and sailing type of lifeboat, primitive equipment for tough conditions in which the boat crews of old worked wonders. The 1930s saw the widespread use of the familiar motor lifeboat which has become the trade mark of today's lifeboatman in the eye of the general public. Braunton and Morte Bay Stations were closed in the early years of this century, and Lynmouth, Watchet and Burnham followed in the 1930s. After the war, improved motor lifeboats of the Oakley and Watson types maintained the service but a revolutionary development in the late sixties was to change the public image of the old lifeboats, even though the spirit of the service was to remain as efficient and undaunted as ever. In 1968 there arrived on the Clovelly station the first of the new cruising type of lifeboat, manned by a professional crew, that operates on a permanent cruising basis in the waters it is allocated. Numbered 70-001, the R.N.L.B. *Charles H. Barrett* was the 35th lifeboat given by the Civil Service, a formidable seventy foot vessel, packed with the latest navigation, radar and rescue aids, and capable of speeds of eleven knots or so in a Force 8 as she proved in service. A later vessel of this type was named *City of Bristol* and a public appeal in support of her cost was launched in the city. This boat represented the R.N.L.I. at the Silver Jubilee Review of the Fleet by Her Majesty Queen Elizabeth II at Spithead in June 1977. Today the lifeboats remain the mainstay of the rescue services at sea, but the role of the helicopter is advancing all the while. It has advantages of speed and mobility over the lifeboat, although limited to operations in daylight. The helicopters of No. 22 Squadron R.A.F. based at Chivenor in North Devon and those of the Fleet Air Arm Station at Yeovilton in Somerset have played a splendid part in West of England rescue work in recent years.

Bristol Channel seamen from previous centuries did not have the benefit of modern technology and they suffered casualities annually in the never-ending struggle with the sea. Above all other coastlines in Britain, the Channel is no place for the inexperienced or indecisive navigator, and even the expert can be unlucky. So the record of shipwreck down the centuries is an extensive one. An average winter gale, like that of the first week of April 1899, would account for anything up to a dozen small traders or fishing boats. In that particular storm, four went down off Lundy alone. Among the small wrecks there would be regular losses of larger ships, storms being the most prevalent cause.

Two of the most tragic and spectacular wrecks in the Channel occurred on opposite shores at the entrance and both were due to the overwhelming power of the sea. H.M.S. *Weazle,* 200 tons, was a twelve gun brig that was on an anti-privateer duty in the winter of 1798/99, based on Appledore and under the command of the Hon. Henry Grey, son of Lord Stamford. French privateers in the approaches to Bristol were a constant preoccupation of Bristol merchants at this period of the war with the revolutionaries, and a request for regular patrols had gone from the city to the First Lord of the Admiralty, Lord Spencer. On February 10th, 1799, the brig left Appledore to patrol the north coasts of Devon and Cornwall and eventually put into Falmouth. That evening a violent storm struck the *Weazle* and she attempted to find shelter to the lee of Baggy Point but went ashore 200 yards south of headland. The entire company of 106 people on board were drowned, and only a single body was recovered at the time. This turned out to be that of a woman named Nancy Golding, and as the crew had taken part in a convivial farewell party before the ship left Appledore, there were those who explained the unauthorised presence of a woman in a ship on active service by saying that the loss was due to excess drinking on board. Later a further twenty-five bodies were recovered from the sea.

The other spectacular Channel wreck belongs to the twentieth century and demonstrates that all modern aids cannot stave off the power of the sea if navigational errors are made. On April 23rd, 1947, the American built Liberty ship *Samtampa,* owned by the British Government and managed by Houlder Bros. Ltd., was on passage from Middlesbrough to Newport when her engines failed and she went aground on Sker Point near Porthcawl in a south-westerly gale. The Mumbles lifeboat (Coxswain William Gammon) went to her assistance but was unable to locate her and returned to get further information. The lifeboat then sailed again into the eye of the storm. There are no eye-witnesses to what occurred thereafter, but as the storm abated, the lifeboat was seen capsized and empty nearby, and the *Samtampa* lay on her side abandoned. Eight lifeboatmen and thirty-nine crew members died in the incident from which there were no survivors.

The upper Channel and the river mouth can be equally dangerous, and here quite often people who would not consider themselves seafarers were caught up in the wrecks. In April 1855 a party of Gloucestershire farmers left Sharpness in the sloop *Despatch* to spend a day at Chepstow market on the other side of the Severn. The day's trading was good and *Despatch* sailed on her return journey with about forty people, twenty sheep, thirty-six pigs, seven cows and a horse. The deep water channel crosses from the Welsh to the English side hereabouts, and, due to bad weather, the fairway was missed and *Despatch* ws driven aground on the sandbanks below Aust Cliffs, near present-day Severn Beach. All on board were lost except for seven hardy souls who literally clung for their lives to the seven cattle who swam safely ashore!

Fortunately, not all our local shipwrecks have involved loss of life and this was so in the most publicised of all, the loss of the battleship H.M.S. *Montague* which grounded on Lundy in thick fog at 2.00 a.m. on May

The old English and Welsh Grounds Lightship ended her days as a floating clubhouse in Bathurst Basin, Bristol.

30th, 1906. All attempts to get her off were a failure and she was broken up where she lay. The only loss suffered by the Navy was its reputation (the officers thought they had grounded on Hartland) and the unfortunate Captain and his navigator were court-martialled.

The safety record of the Bristol Channel pleasure steamers is impressive. In their heyday, the Bristol paddle steamers never lost a fare-paying passenger through wreck or accident. Although small, the paddlers were built like little battleships in order to withstand the wear-and-tear of this business, and most of them were good seaboats. So, even if the passengers turned several shades of green, they usually arrived on time and always in safety. The one hazard that could always halt the paddlers was fog and in the early years of this century, before the days of radar, it was responsible for two spectacular pile-ups, fortunately without injury to ship or human.

On Easter Monday, April 1st, 1907, the 6.40 a.m. steamer from Newport to Bristol was Campbells' *Albion*. She left on time in good weather but ran into fog on the Bristol side, which had already caused all the Bristol sailings to be cancelled, hundreds being turned away from Hotwells Pontoon. Captain Webber of the *Albion* pressed on at reduced speed, and after groping around for a while, the ship ground to a halt on Black Nore Point, Portishead, right in front of the Nautical School! None of the 400 Welshmen on board were hurt and they went on to Bristol by rail. It took the combined efforts of seven tugs to pull *Albion* free on the evening tide. Nineteen years later the same company's *Cambria* went ashore on July 12th, 1926 at Rilledge Point, two miles east of Ilfracombe, while groping her way to the resort in fog. Captain Livingstone ordered his passengers aft in an attempt to raise the bows and float off, but *Cambria* was stuck fast. In the best tradition of the sea, the women and children were put off in the boats, and Ilfracombe lifeboat helped transfer the rest to the *Glen Usk*. The *Cambria* floated off on the next tide and another potential disaster had been prevented by stout construction and a little bit of luck.

The *Glen Usk,* the paddle steamer that went to the aid of the *Cambria* in the incident just related, was herself in the headlines thirty-three years later when she went aground in the Avon at the Horseshoe Bend on August 30th, 1959, while outward bound for Cardiff with 600 passengers on board. Again there was no damage to vessel or complement, although some passengers gathered a little of the famous Avon mud as they were led ashore.

It is in the five miles of the river that lead from Avonmouth up to Bristol that some of the more sensational Bristol shipwrecks have happened. The Avon at this point has always demanded careful navigation and the river pilots have developed a set of rules over the years that only the rash or the fogbound will disobey. The chances are that the river will always win in this kind of gamble, because basic rule no. 1 is that the passage either way should never be made on a tide that is past high water. The possible consequences of a wreck in the Avon on the trade of the city if the river remained blocked for any length of time was a constant worry to the Corporation, and at several times in the history of the Port of Bristol, the unthinkable has happened. Even in 1970, when it was discussing the imminent return to Bristol of the s.s. *Great Britain,* the Docks Committee gave earnest and lengthy consideration to the possibility of the old ship being wrecked in the Avon and blocking what little trade was left in the City Docks. As the author, who was present, can testify, it was felt that £1 million insurance cover was hardly enough to guard against possible mishap.

Absurd as it may now seem to the general reader to insist on such a provision (£1 million was a goodly sum in 1970), the Docks Committee were arguing from the sum of centuries of bitter experience. Long before, their forebears in 1579 had to deal with the problem of the *Lion,* a merchantman laden with salt and oil that struck rocks in Hungroad and sank. This was in March and the Corporation immediately called in a number of ships' captains to effect salvage. They struggled for weeks without success and the by now distraught Mayor and Corporation were appealing to the Queen and the Privy Council, apparently with no result. Then in May the wreck was pulled to the surface and brought ashore. Then it slipped back down the river bank and the blockage became worse than before. The tough timbers had to be broken up where they lay and the port was only opened again in March 1580.

The blockage in 1579 is probably the longest in the history of the port but the danger was always present. The nineteenth century had several incidents and none more famous than the wreck of the *Demerara,* at the time the largest ship built with the exception of the *Great Britain.* The *Demerara* was a new paddle steamer of 3,000 tons, built by William Patterson for the West India Mail Steamship Company and launched on September 27th, 1851. On November 10th of that year, she left Cumberland Basin, Bristol, in charge of a Glasgow tug, to be towed to the Clyde to have her engines fitted. She was late for the tide which was ebbing fast. The tow set off at the dangerously high speed of eight knots to make up time. After a protest by Patterson, who was on board, speed was slackened but the ship was difficult to control and she struck the Clifton bank about a quarter of a mile below the as yet uncompleted Suspension Bridge. The tide swung the ship across the Avon, and soon left her high and dry, effectively blocking the port. In the night that followed, as the tide rose, thousands gathered on the riverside to watch frenzied salvage efforts by torchlight which almost succeeded until the *Demerara* slid once more across the stream. She was eventually refloated and completed as a sailing ship, the *British Empire,* after being abandoned to underwriters as a total wreck, following the Avon incident.

Another incident was the grounding of the Liverpool ship *Refuge* outside the Cumberland Basin entrance at Rownham on March 13th, 1854, which closed the port for three days until she was floated off. A more serious affair took place on the night tide of Sunday May 12th, 1878, when the Waterford steamer *Gipsy,* 691 tons, outward bound for her home port grounded near Black Rock. A tug failed to tow her off and her passengers were taken off. On the next tide, she was forced across the stream and broke her back, completely blocking the fairway. She was unloaded as she lay and on the 17th, a Royal Navy and Royal Engineers party blew the wreck up. But it was not until June 4th, after further demolition work, that the river was re-opened. Earlier in the decade, the Docks Commmittee had received a similar shock when a German steamer *Kron Prinz* 800 tons, had grounded and capsized in Sea Mills Reach. They were relieved when it was discovered that the wreck did not block the river, but it took three weeks to salvage. Later on, Hill's *Llandaff City* also blocked the river.

Without the modern aid of radar, finding one's way down the fog bound river must have been akin to the stepping out of a blindfolded man along a greased and bent pole with no chance of turning back. So it must have seemed to Captain White of the Glasgow steamer *Ettrick,* 513 tons, when he left Hotwells in the small hours of Saturday September 6th, 1924, and immediately ran into fog in the river. *Ettrick* was a regular caller at Bristol and linked the city with Glasgow. She was loaded with chocolates and cigarettes and eight passengers were on board. *Ettrick* managed to find her way as far as the Bristol side of the Horseshoe Bend, and then grounded. Passengers and crew scuttled ashore, the mud and the ebb tide left the ship capsized in the river, again blocking up the City Docks. Among the blockaded vessels was the paddle steamer *Britannia,* booked that morning to take football fans to watch Cardiff City in the first round of the F.A. Cup!

Crowds flocked to Sea Mills to gape at the plight of the little ship—and to help themselves to her cargo, which was beginning to float ashore. More then twenty appeared in court on the Monday morning and were fined £5 each. One boatman, caught landing a cane chair, twelve pairs of boots and seven sacks of flour, explained that he 'found them floating in the river'. A benevolent bench acquitted him!

The *Ettrick* lay in the river for six weeks, while salvage experts led by the late Mr. Harry Brown struggled to raise her, although ships were allowed to edge past after three weeks as the *Ettrick's* upperworks had been removed. Finally. on October 25th, *Ettrick* was refloated and, with Pilot Cooper astride her bows and Captain White sitting on the site of his demolished bridge, she was towed to Rownham and beached.

But Bristolians have seen disaster even closer to the centre of their city than the river. We have already mentioned the boiler explosion on the *Black Eagle* in 1866. A similar explosion blew up the *Red Rover,* one of the Harbour 'penny steamers', as she was about to leave Cumberland Basin for the Drawbridge with fifty passengers on the evening of July 22nd, 1850. Fifteen people died and the harbour steamers lost considerable support, to the evident satisfaction of the local cabbies.

Another harbour disaster was the sinking at her moorings of the Bristol Steam Navigation Company's coaster *Cato* when she was rammed by the Ellerman liner *City of Brooklyn* at 'P' Shed, Avonmouth on 24th April 1963. What should have been a normal docking became a nightmare when the *City of Brooklyn's* engines failed to go astern at a vital moment. The crew got ashore safely but the *Cato* was a total loss. She was raised by T. R. Brown & Sons and scrapped at Newport.

To bring the story of Bristol Channel shipwrecks up to date, as this book was going to press in the summer of 1981, there came news of the loss of the excursion motor-vessel *Prince Ivanhoe* on the Glamorgan coast at Portheynon, west of Mumbles. *Prince Ivanhoe* was the former British Railways ferry *Shanklin,* 986 tons, built at Dumbarton and employed on the Portsmouth–Ryde I.o.W. route. She was bought in the winter of 1980 by the Firth of Clyde Steam Packet Co. Ltd., as a back-up vessel and running mate to the well known paddler *Waverley,* operated by a non-profit making preservation society. Following the withdrawal of Channel excursions by P. & A. Campbell Ltd., at the end of the 1979 season, and the single season of 1980 operated by Campbells for the Landmark Trust, it was decided to operate *Prince Ivanhoe* in the Bristol Channel in 1981.

On her first Bristol visit on May 1st, the *Ivanhoe* struck a rock in the

The Cato *seen from the old Tobacco Wharf, moored at Wapping East.* Cato *was sunk at Avonmouth in 1963.*

Avon and sustained damage which was to cause her to spend two weeks in dry dock at Barry. Later there was an incident when she struck fishing vessels as she entered Minehead. Then, on August 3rd, while operating a sailing from Penarth to Minehead, Mumbles and the Gower coast, she struck rocks off Portheynon and filled rapidly. Her Captain beached her at Portheynon, and 400 passengers were taken off by the local lifeboat, the ship's own boats and life-rafts, and RAF helicopters. One elderly passenger died of a heart attack during the rescue operation, but there were no other casualties. The sea had again demanded its toll.

So the perpetual struggle between man and the sea continues as the twenty-first century approaches. As each new safety device is introduced, the margin of security at sea increases. Yet hold-fires present the same serious challenge and there are still the odd cases of vessels vanishing without trace. Fortunately, there have been no cases of that happening to a Bristol ship for many years, but of all the maritime disasters, this must surely be the worst for those ashore to face. Imagine the dreadful uncertainty of weeks of concern before the final admission of loss. Such a situation was faced by the relatives of the crew of the first *Bristol City*, 1,725 tons and A1 at Lloyds, which sailed from New York for Bristol on December 28th, 1890 and was never heard from again.

P. & A. Campbell's paddle steamer Ravenswood *as she appeared when built in 1891.*

RAVENSWOOD
FRANK SHIPSIDES 1981

SEA PRINCE
SEA PRINCE
— FRANK SHIPSIDES — 1951

The m.v. Prince Ivanhoe *(ex* Shanklin*), Bristol-based pleasure steamer which sank off Portheynon in July 1981.*

The Royal Yacht Victoria and Albert *at the opening of the Royal Edward Dock on July 9th, 1908.*

'Praise God, now, for an English war
The grey tide and the sullen coast
The menace of the urgent hour
The single island, like a tower
Ringed with an angry host.

When from the Cinque Ports and the Wight
From Plymouth Sound and Bristol Town
There comes a noise that breaks out sleep
Of the deep calling to the deep
Where the ships go up and down.'

Dorothy L. Sayers—*The English War.*

A 'River' Class Frigate of World War II, Bristol-built.

The Port of Bristol at War (1914–1945)

THE WAR that burst over continental Europe in August 1914 took most Bristolians by surprise, although, like many of their fellow countrymen, they had expected to clash at some time or other with the expansionist empire of Kaiser Wilhelm II. But when the realisation that war with Germany was a certainty, the P.B.A. responded quickly to Government plans to hurriedly dispatch a British Expeditionary Force to France. While most of the army personnel crossed to France from English Channel ports, Avonmouth became a major supply port with ships running around Land's End to Le Havre, Cherbourg and St. Nazaire. The first military stores began to arrive at Avonmouth on August 1st, and by the time war was declared at midnight on August 4th, many of the transit sheds were full to capacity and hundreds of tons of supplies were stacked in the open.

At this same hour, the city's adopted ship, the light cruiser H.M.S. *Bristol* was cruising north of the Bahamas, bound from Jamaica for Newfoundland. At noon on August 6th, Captain Fanshawe of the *Bristol* received orders from Admiral Cradock, C-in-C West Indies, to turn south to intercept the German cruiser *Karlsruhe,* which was making for the open

Atlantic, with commerce raiding as her objective. The German ship was larger and faster than *Bristol* but this did not deter Fanshawe and his crew as they steered to head her off. *Karlsruhe* was sighted in brillant moonlight, but she did not see *Bristol* until Fanshawe opened fire at 7,000 yards range, putting the cruiser into the history books as the first British warship to go into action in World War I. Hopes of victory faded, however, as the German ship used her superior speed to escape under cover of smoke. H.M.S. *Bristol* was to spend a busy war. On December 8th, 1914 she was part of Admiral Sturdee's squadron that defeated the German cruisers under Graf von Spee at the battle of the Falkland Islands. *Bristol* had been suffering slight engine trouble and was at anchor with her fires out and both engines opened up, when the German ships were first sighted from the islands, at eight in the morning. By some miracle of exertion, *Bristol's* engineers got her into action by 10.30 and she sank the German supply ships *Baden* and *Santa Isabel.* Later in the war, *Bristol* served in the Mediterranean and was finally paid off in 1920. During her short career, which began in February 1911 at the famous Clydebank yard of John Brown, the 4,800 ton cruiser had added the battle honours 'Falklands 1914' and 'Adriatic 1917' to the other ten already held by H.M. ships named *Bristol*.

Back in Avonmouth, thirty-six ships had arrived in the first weeks of the war to take some part of the B.E.F. to France. A Royal Proclamation had given the Admiralty authority to take over ships at will, and they used their powers to some purpose. Contemporary records show that there was, nevertheless, a shortage of ships, and a desperate port General Manager had to plead with the War Office to hold back supplies and men until more ships arrived. In the meanwhile, he ordered supplies to be stacked outside the docks in unfinished St. Andrews Road, which in those days led north to nowhere, and allowed waiting soldiers to use the unfinished northern end of the Royal Edward Dock for nude bathing.

Fortunately for the P.B.A. Bristol had an agreement with the Army, dating from 1910, that Crown Ships and cargoes should be charged at current rates less one third. This worked out at 6d per ton and the Port quietly began to send in its bills to the Government. Other less fortunate ports came under the Harbours Act of 1847 which rules that all Crown vessels and cargoes could have free use of any dock or harbour in the country. The Government took full advantage of the Act until February 1916, when a group of almost bankrupt dock undertakings persuaded Prime Minister Asquith to change his mind.

In the first two months of the war, 4,600 troops left Avonmouth for France. Within days of arrival, some of them stood in the path of the German Army at Mons, gaining valuable time for the French to re-group and eventually to hold von Kluck on the Marne.

Once again Bristol had become a leading port of the Empire. Her shipping lines and businesses took their full part in the national effort and

The Royal Edward *of the Canadian Northern Line, ran with her sister,* Royal George, *to Canada from Avonmouth, 1910–1914.* Royal Edward *was lost in World War I.*

both Bristol and Avonmouth Docks busied themselves with the concerns of war. Soon the casualties began. The liner services of the Canadian Northern Line ended in October. On her final voyage, the *Royal George* arrived with 1,200 men of the Canadian Army. This was the last that

Avonmouth would see of the smart 'Royals' in their peacetime role. Both became troopships and in 1915 sailed out of the port with troops bound for the Aegean Sea and the Dardanelles campaign. The *Royal Edward* became an early victim of the campaign. On August 18th, 1915, she was torpedoed by UB-14 at the entrance to the Aegean, six miles west of Kandelinisa island. 935 lives were lost, including 132 of the ship's crew, most of whom came from the Bristol area and had signed on at Avonmouth. *Royal George* survived the war to acquire the dignity of a Cunarder before being scrapped in 1922.

Although German surface raiders had been rounded up by the Royal Navy in the first six months of the war, the year 1915 saw the rise of the submarine as a weapon in the commercial war at sea. Bristol ship owners got a nasty shock when the trader *Bengrove* was torpedoed without warning twenty-five miles east of Lundy and five miles out from Ilfracombe. This was only forty miles west of Flatholm and, although no other ship was lost so far east again, it showed what the U-boats could do.

Bristol seamen, and the world, were shown exactly what unrestricted submarine warfare meant when, on May 7th, the Cunard record-breaker *Lusitania,* inward bound for Liverpool, was sunk without warning off Old Head of Kensale by U-20 and 1,198 people drowned. Two months later, on August 19th, the Bristol City Line's largest vessel, the 2,970 ton *New York City* was sunk by a U-boat forty-four miles south east of the Fastnet while outward bound from the City Docks for New York. Fortunately there was no loss of life.

Some ships were more fortunate. On the same day that the *New York City* went down, the Leyland liner *Nicosian* was saved by the Q-ship H.M.S. *Baralong* which caught U-27 in the act and sank her. Another U-boat sprayed the transport *Anglo-Californian* with bullets, killing the captain and twenty of his crew until chased off by two destroyers. Three other ships, including another Leyland liner *Armenian,* were sunk around Lundy in 1915, but then a lull ensued that lasted throughout 1916.

The relative safety of Avonmouth meant that thousands of Dominion troops passed through the port during the war years on their way to the front in France. So Bristol welcomed the sons and grandsons of emigrants she had sent overseas in earlier years. As 1916 ended, the U-boats were back in the Bristol Channel. The New Year saw the crescendo of the

U-boat campaign when the Germans had over eighty submarines in commission. They were Germany's one chance of victory and she determined to take it. They sank thirty-five ships in January and followed with February figures of 86,103 tons, climaxing in April with 156 vessels totalling half a million tons of shipping. All this cost only twelve U-boats and Germany was within a hair's breadth of starving Britain out. Food rationing was introduced and Bristol's maritime trade declined. Tonnages were a million down on pre-war figures. Then, at last, a tardy Admiralty introduced the convoy system, a well tried device last used in the Napoleonic Wars, and losses began to decline. Bristol Channel convoys gathered at the assembly point off Milford Haven and sailed, usually in groups of ten or twelve, under naval escort. The crisis was over, but the losses had been severe. Sinkings continued in the Channel right through to the end of the war.

Charles Hill & Sons Ltd. had replaced the *New York City* by the *Boston City*, built at Albion Dockyard and placed in service in February 1917. She completed five round voyages to New York from the City Docks, but was lost on the sixth trip, outward bound with a cargo of China clay, being torpedoed off St. Anne's Head, Pembrokeshire. The worst incident of all was the callous sinking of the clearly marked hospital ship *Glenart Castle* in broad daylight ten miles off Lundy on February 6th, 1918, when fifty-eight wounded patients went down in their beds.

While ships went down, Bristol played its part in the vital struggle to build replacements. Hill's Albion Dockyard was constantly busy, launching wartime standard ships with such unlovely names as *War Damson* and *War Plum*. The last months of the war were not happy ones in the port. Although trade was depressed, labour was short and proposals to use the Army's Transport Battalion provoked inevitable protest from the dockers. It took all the skills of a rising young union official called Ernest Bevin to prevent an all-out strike.

But at last it was all over and although November 11th, 1918 was a damp, drizzle-filled day, the dockers went home at 11.00 a.m. They returned the following day, characteristically demanding to be paid for their absence. They were.

It was time to take stock. Every Bristol-based shipping company had lost ships. Bristol Steam Navigation Co. lost their *Argo* and four others from a pre-war fleet of eleven. In addition to other losses already mentioned, Bristol City Line lost *Kansas City* and *Bristol City*. With other lines it was much the same. Soon replacements were on the slipways and the docks began to receive record numbers of ships for repair. Slowly, trade came back. Then, as if to signal that peace had finally come, the paddle steamers returned.

The little excursion ships, with their shallow draught and good handling qualities, proved to be excellent minesweepers and *Devonia* and *Brighton Queen* had left Bristol as early as September 1914. By the end of July 1915, the entire Campbell fleet, with Bristol crews, was serving in the drab grey colour of the Royal Navy. Mostly they served in the North Sea and on one occasion were alleged to have been mistaken for light cruisers by one German commander! The *Barry* actually got all the way out to Gallipoli and claimed to be the last British ship away from the beaches when Churchill's ill-judged venture was ended by the War Cabinet. Two of the paddlers, *Brighton Queen* and *Lady Ismay* were mined off the Belgium coast in 1915 and did not return, although the crews of both ships were rescued.

Bristol's trade had suffered during the war and she now faced a period of reconstruction. The building of the Royal Edward Dock had provided six years of increasing trade from 1908–14, and had enabled the P.B.A. to stand four demanding years of war. While little expansion was possible in the crowded area around the City Docks, at Avonmouth plans went ahead to double granary space, extend the oil basin and build the Royal Edward cold store to accept the frozen products of the Australian Commonwealth and South America. The same vision that had caused Bristol to build the Royal Edward Dock now re-asserted itself and plans went ahead. As the years passed so plans came to fruition. Trade which in 1914 stood at 3,750,000 tons annually had fallen to 2,250,000 tons in 1919.

By 1928, it was back to 3,300,000 and the Eastern Arm of the Royal Edward Dock was completed. It was opened by the Prince of Wales. New transit sheds sprang up in the City Docks and by 1939 trade was near the 4,000,000 tons mark. This included 6,115,000 stems of bananas, a figure that was never to be exceeded, 946,000 tons of oil products and 355,000 tons of timber in its various forms.

Despite the depression of the early 1930s Bristol between the wars was a vibrant booming city. Although unemployment and bad housing were found here as in other parts of Britain, there does not seem to have been the hopeless sense of despair that was felt in the North East and South Wales. Indeed, the new industries around Bristol, particularly the emerging aircraft plants, drew many Welsh migrants eager for jobs. For a population that had quadrupled in a century (in 1851 it was 137,000 but by 1930 over 400,000) the accommodation of the vast number of new Bristolians could no longer be contained in the bounds of the old city. A large boundary extension took place in 1935 and the first attempts at town planning came in.

In these inter-war years, there began the first stirrings of that upheaval that was to change entirely the pattern of the city and destroy the old Bristol for ever. Right up to 1914, the city had been contained largely around its port, and thousands of small working class homes, many of them slums, had crouched around the city centre and docks, backing on factories, and warehouses; the whole a human ant-heap of commercial activity. A growing awareness of human dignity and the basic right of all to share in prosperity led to serious attempts after the 1914–18 war to provide workers' homes fit to live in with decent surroundings. 'Slum clearance' was the central slogan in political jargon of the 1920s and 1930s. New housing estates sprang up in Sea Mills, Horfield, Filton and Knowle in green, healthy countryside. As people moved out, so fast buses were needed to take them to their work, into the city or out to Filton and Avonmouth. The old, reliable but slow trams could not cope with the new demands and Bristol's last trams ran in 1939. The same year work proceeded apace on covering the Frome between St. Augustines Parade and Broad Quay. By 1940 buses were running above the waters that had been of such service to Bristol since 1247.

Yet Bristol never possessed a real 'dockland', an area distinct from the city centre which became a cosmopolitan sailors' quarter like Cardiff's Tiger Bay, where the police went in pairs on a Saturday night. The brothels and doss-houses of other great ports never developed in Bristol, and while there were some rowdy pubs in King Street and along Welsh Back and Bathurst Basin, it was rare for fists to fly and knives to be drawn. Some historians put this down to the hold that non-conformist religion had on nineteenth century Bristol, but another reason must be that ships

Hotwells seen from Baltic Wharf. Royal Naval Reserve drill ships have used Mardyke Wharf during the nineteenth and twentieth centuries.

trading out of the port were usually crewed by Bristol men who, when they signed off, simply went home.

So Bristol pursued its business of a great international port as the years sped by. Even big P. & O. cruise ships, like *Strathmore,* called at Bristol. Mostly it was a steady routine, interrupted on occasion by events such as that on the evening of November 1st, 1929, when a sudden fog caught eleven ships on passage in the Avon. The flotilla included two Bristol City liners, *New York City* and *Bristol City*. Masters and pilots could only wait helpless as ships crashed into each other on the river bank, and then began to settle on the falling tide. As dawn broke on the following morning, and the tide began to make again, the Avon presented a grim sight of stranded vessels. The *Bristol City* had turned through 180 degrees—something thought impossible in that narrow waterway and was supporting a semi-capsized tramp, laden with a cargo of resin and turpentine. The wonder of the incident is that not a single vessel or life was lost. Others were not so lucky. The sea still demanded its toll, as in January 1933, when the *Exeter City* was caught in a storm off Cape Race, Newfoundland. A wave tore away the entire bridge together with the master, the O.O.W., the coxswain and a look-out. Only an alert radio operator, and the skill of the crew of a nearby American ship prevented the other twenty-two members of the crew from following them.

Bristol had fought the 1914–18 war on the oceans. The second round with Germany which began on September 3rd, 1939 was to be a very different affair. In the earlier war, Bristol was safely tucked away on the west coast. Even if the U-boats operated down-channel, the port itself was a safe haven. All that changed in 1939, as Goering's Luftwaffe went into action and every square inch of the British Isles came to recognise the black crosses that stood out like the mark of doomsday on the wings of Heinkels, Dorniers and Junkers.

The U-boats came first, nevertheless. With the war only two weeks old, U-29 struck west of Lundy and sent the large aircraft carrier, H.M.S. *Courageous* to the bottom. U-boats would remain in the Western Approaches and the entrance to the Bristol Channel for the entire war and many Bristol ships would perish from their torpedoes. Typical were the wartime activities of the Bristol City Line, which suffered heavily at the hands of Admiral Doenitz's marauders. *Toronto City,* 2,500 g.r.t. was on weather service duties when lost with all hands in July 1941. *Montreal City,* 3,000 g.r.t. went down when a U-boat picked her off as a convoy scattered in bad weather in December 1942. Again there were no survivors. *Bristol City* was hit by two torpedoes in a convoy on the night of May 5th, 1943 and went down in under ten minutes. Fifteen crew members died, but the master and twenty-seven others were rescued by a R.N. corvette.

Another Bristol ship, *Gloucester City* went to the aid of survivors of the convoy attacked by the pocket battleship *Admiral Scheer* on Guy Fawkes Day 1940, when the merchant cruiser H.M.S. *Jervis Boy* heroically sacrificed herself to save her charges. In the southerly gale that blew that night, *Gloucester City* almost rammed a large warship that loomed up out of the wind and spray. To this day, the crew swear it was the *Admiral Scheer*!

Once again, the Campbell paddle steamers had gone to war, eight of them for the second time, the first four being taken over on September 13th 1939. Some suffered a change of name to avoid confusion with other R.N. ships. So *Britannia* became *Skiddaw, Cambria* was *Plynlimmon* and

The light cruiser H.M.S. Bristol *of 1910. She was the sixth warship of the Royal Navy to carry the name, and first British ship to go into action in World War I.*

Waverley renamed *Snaefell*. Such was Their Lordships' preoccupation with mountains.

Crewed by Bristol men, the paddlers reached their apotheosis of glory in the drama of the Dunkirk evacuation, May 24th to June 1st, 1940. Eight of the steamers went to the beaches and brought away thousands of soldiers. Three did not return. *Brighton Belle* struck the wreck of another ship, and *Brighton Queen* and *Devonia* were destroyed by German bombers. Two more paddlers, *Waverley* and *Glen Avon* were lost later in the war, two were scrapped as worn out, and only *Britannia, Glen Usk* and *Ravenswood* returned to Bristol to take up the holiday trade once more.

Meanwhile, the Port of Bristol had gone to war. Avonmouth became a principal petroleum importing centre, and four million tons annually became routine. Much of it went to fuel the aircraft that won the Battle of Britain, and to the growing fleet of Bomber Command. Throughout these early months of the war, while Hitler made Europe his own, there was an uneasy feeling that the wrath had yet to come. A full black-out had been ordered in 1939, shelters built and sandbags filled, while most male civilians not in the forces were holding essential war-time jobs either in A.R.P. or the Home Guard.

Bristol had to endure sporadic air raids through the summer of 1940. The first raid came in the early hours of June 25th, when five people were killed, but the worst so far had been on Filton on September 25th when Heinkel 111s attacked the B.A.C. and did considerable damage causing many deaths.

The real blow fell on November 24th. In six hours of destruction, Kesselring's III Luftflötte, based in France, tore the heart out of Bristol, as the old town around Bristol Bridge succumbed to a hail of high explosives and incendiaries. The City Docks area was damaged and Charles Hill's shipyard hit. Two hundred people died. Hill's were hit again in the next raid on December 2nd, and part of the quayside at Welsh Back collapsed. Four nights later, six factories in the City Dock area were hit, and the old Merchants Hall destroyed. The port stayed at work despite the raids, ships continued to arrive and depart and—sure sign of Government anxiety—King George VI toured the damaged areas on December 16th. The New Year of 1941 opened with a sharp attack on January 3rd/4th when the City Docks granary was destroyed, but Avonmouth was left unmolested until April 9th/10th when a cinema was hit, but all vital installations in the port survived.

The City Docks were a target two nights later in the attack that came to be known as the 'Good Friday Raid'. Hits were scored in Canon's Marsh and Broad Quay. 180 people died but it was to be the last heavy raid on the port during the war. True, the horror of the Broad Weir bus raid of August 28th, 1942 had yet to come and the Luftwaffe's last effort in 1944. By the summer of 1941, Bristol was over the worst. She had suffered seventy-six attacks and 1,299 had died with another 2,602 injured. But when the enemy had done his worst, Bristol was still there and through the war years to 1945 would go on playing her part. Great quantities of war materials passed through the port, the Americans arrived and left their own indelible mark on the city. General Omar Bradley sketched out his plans for D-day in the hallowed precincts of Clifton College, while in 1944, four and threequarter million tons of petroleum passed through Avonmouth.

In Albion Dockyard, history repeated itself as once again, frigates for the Royal Navy slid into the Floating Harbour. In all, twenty-six frigates, corvettes, boom defence vessels, landing craft and patrol boats left Messrs. Charles Hill & Sons' yards for the Allied fleets.

The war ended on a confident note. The port had survived and grown. It had shown it could handle trade far beyond what was expected of it. Never had it handled so many ships as in these war years. It is no wonder that it faced the coming peace with renewed confidence.

A frigate fitting out at Albion Dockyard during World War II.

'Green upon the flooded Avon shore the after-storm-wet sky
Quick the struggling withy branches let the leaves of autumn fly
And a star shone over Bristol, wonderfully far and high.'

John Betjeman—*Bristol*

H.M.Y. Britannia *at Royal Portbury Dock, August 8th, 1977.*

Ending or Beginning? (1945–1981)

To the returning servicemen in 1945, the port of Bristol seemed much the same as the one they had left six years before. The busy, self-confident life of the docks was vibrant as ever. Coasters called in at the City Docks again, and cargoes came and went as before from Princes Wharf, Canons Marsh and Wapping. The Scandinavian timber boats were back at Baltic Wharf and, joy of joys, the *Ravenswood* took Campbell's first post-war excursion out of Hotwells on April 15th, 1946. The queue of intending passengers had stretched a quarter of a mile along the Portway.

Albion Dockyard was busy with new orders, mainly for craft built for special purposes. Typical were a Trinity House light and buoy, a lightship for Ireland, numerous dredging craft including the Port Authority's triple grab vessel *Clifton,* and a variety of tugs from the small to large ocean going salvage vessels.

At Avonmouth and in the City docks, trade fell off somewhat as the war ended. Then the impetus of the post-war export drive with its emphasis on dollar earning drove the figures upwards once more. Bristol still looked westward, and thousands of Midlands-built motor vehicles went out through Avonmouth for Canada and the U.S. By 1951 trade had reached its war-time level of 5½ million tons and in the next decade it would reach a total of 7½ millions by 1961. Continuous improvement took place at Avonmouth.

During the latter years of the 1940s, the port received its final trading visits from large sailing ships. On October 12th, 1948, the four-masted barque *Passat* docked with wheat from Australia. She had made the passage in 143 days. She had been part of the fleet of Captain Gustaf Erikson, the Finn from the Aland Islands who ran the world's last line of sailing ships.

While the port prospered, so the city expanded in the immediate post-war years. There was a critical housing shortage as old homes had been destroyed or worn out, and the population swollen with war-time workers who came to remain. Housing became the first priority and great new estates arose on the city boundaries at Hartcliffe, Withywood, Bishopsworth, Lawrence Weston, Henbury and Lockleaze. This was the age of the 'pre-fab'—the temporary bungalow built to last ten years but destined in some cases to last more than three times as long.

Whereas houses arose in their thousands, the amenities that turn estates into communities were not always forthcoming, and even today many are lacking. Additionally, even if progress was made in the suburbs, where for example, over 23,000 new school places had been provided by 1963, rebuilding the central areas was woefully slow, and often such proposals as were made by the City Council provoked controversy of one form or another. At the centre of the arguments was the road pattern, as the City's Planning Department strove to deal with ten per cent annual rate of increase in the number of cars on Bristol's streets. Paramount among the problems were, as ever, the river crossings, and both Bath and Bedminster Bridges were duplicated, the former in 1960 and the latter in 1963. The old swing bridge over the Junction Cut at Cumberland Basin was superseded by an impressive replacement, centrepiece of the Cumberland Basin Scheme. This was completed in 1965 (there were red faces when the bridge stuck fast and refused to swing at the opening ceremony) and much of the old Hotwells scene was demolished to make way for the approach roads. In all the scheme cost £2,650,000. Bristolians have been ambivalent in their view of the scheme. It certainly cleared the traffic jams (until a departing sand boat causes a bridge swing in the rush hour!) and even won a Civic Trust Award for its layout and landscaping. But it took away part of old Bristol.

Other more radical causes and their effects lay ahead for the port. Changes in ship design and cargo handling now began to appear. The super-tanker was a creature of the early 1960s and she was followed by the large bulk carrier and the container ship. Only a few people realised that a maritime revolution was at hand, and even they were to be astonished at the speed of the changes.

The Passat *at Avonmouth in October 1948. She was the last large sailing ship to deliver a commercial cargo of Australian grain to Bristol.*

The main change was the size of merchant ships. In the ten years from 1961 to 1970, the small coastal ships that brought trade, and therefore profit, to the City Docks virtually disappeared. Similarly, from 1970 onwards, the ocean cargo liner of around 10,000 tons, hundreds of which called at Avonmouth every year, began to be sold for scrap or overseas at the rate of dozens per month. The coastal trade went largely by road, crossing to the Continent in roll-on, roll-off ferries and bringing work in full measure to east coast and English Channel ports which grew even more when Britain entered the E.E.C.

General cargo and even such Bristol staples as refrigerated meat imports began to be containerised and one large container ship might carry as much as five traditional liners.

It was time for change, overdue in fact, and the changes shook Bristol to her foundations, provoked public controversies which outdid those of the nineteenth century, and some of which still await final resolution.

The challenges that faced the City Fathers in 1967 were twofold. First, what must be done about the rapidly vanishing trade of the City Docks? Second, how could Avonmouth handle the large ships of the future, which could not pass through the limited dimensions of the Royal Edward entrance?

By 1970, the City Docks were losing £200,000 annually. The scale of the decline can be judged by the figures for June 1963 when eighty ships berthed in the City Docks as compared with October 1969 when only twenty-eight arrivals were recorded. In 1969 also, the long established Bristol Steam Navigation Company's direct service to Rotterdam and other Continental ports was withdrawn as it was no longer profitable. Services operated by Coast Lines had closed earlier, and the foreign flag vessels, particularly those from the Netherlands had virtually disappeared from the Avon. The only option open to the P.B.A. was closure of the old docks and in this same year of 1969, the City Council promoted a Bill in Parliament which sought powers to end navigation rights in the City Dock system. The proposal was accompanied by a programme of works which would have dammed the New Cut at Ashton and abandoned the Feeder Canal entirely. These latter proposals were aimed at eventually reducing operating costs of the locks.

Immediately, there was a public outcry of the sort so dear to the heart of

Elders & Fyffes Tilapa *nearing Avonmouth with the first post-war cargo of bananas—a sure sign that peace had returned. Shipments had ended in 1940.*

the true Bristolian. The people worst hit were the remaining concerns trading in the docks, the sand interests and Charles Hill & Sons Ltd., the shipbuilders in Albion Dockyard. They promptly entered objections to the Bill and were joined by a strong conservation lobby, prominent among which were the Bristol Civic Society, the Cabot Cruising Club and the Inland Waterways Association. The conservation groups were concerned with the Council's road plans which proposed bridges across the entrance of St. Augustine's Reach and from Cumberland Road across the harbour to join Jacobs Wells Road. Both measures were highly controversial and the conservationists felt that the ending of navigation rights would give the road builders a free hand.

An argumentative Town meeting held at the Colston Hall on December

A typical scene in the City Dock, now long past, with the Stanleigh *seen near Prince Street Bridge.*

15th, 1969 saw the Corporation face their critics in an atmosphere that often descended into uproar. The Bill was decisively rejected. The Council had now no option but to call a Town Poll if they wanted the Bill. This step was taken and a poll called for January 20th, 1970. Both sides took their case to the Bristol electorate. In the event, the Council won, somewhat to their surprise, votes for totalling 22,298 with 16,724 against. So the Bill went to Parliament after all, and the Select Committee of the House of Lords proceeded to apply to the many clauses that establishment's two great contributions to English democracy—restraint and common sense. In the end, the Bill became the Bristol Corporation Act 1971 when Royal Assent was granted on July 27th of that year. As the Queen of Hearts remarked to Alice, everybody had won and everybody had to have prizes. The sand interests had their trade protected and the guarantee of new quays at Avonmouth, the shipyard was guaranteed compensation for closure, the conservation societies achieved their aim of preserving the old waterways and the Corporation got their Bill.

The problem of the future use of the deserted waterways was far from solved, however. The Port Authority rightly considered itself a commercial organisation. By the end of 1972 it was only moving 20,000 tons of cargo in and out of the City Docks and was more than willing to transfer the area to the Planning Committee. The ship building at Albion Dockyard, home of Charles Hill's, launched its last ship *Miranda Guinness* on July 9th, 1976, and then closed its doors at the end of an era that had seen the *Arethusa* and the *Favell*.

In the midst of this withdrawal from the splendours of their city's maritime past, Bristolians received two boosts to their morale which went far to re-kindle the fighting spirit of old.

First, in many ways symbolic of the spirit of the old port, the *Great Britain* came home. We left her in Chapter 5, derelict in Sparrow Cove, an inlet near Port Stanley in the Falkland Islands. There she was abandoned,

The schooner Pascual Flores *under repair in Bristol City Docks in 1980. This is typical of the new uses found for the waterway.*

her only companions the local cormorants and Gentoo penguins, for thirty-three years until her unique antique value began to attract the attention of preservationists. In America Karl Kartum, Director of the San Francisco Maritime Museum, had made two visits to the ship in 1966 and 1967. His trustees supported his proposal to take the *Great Britain* to California. In Britain, the naval architect Ewan Corlett, an authority on the ship and on Brunel, proposed in a letter to *The Times* on November 7th, 1967 that the *Great Britain* was capable of being salvaged and should be returned to this country. The letter prompted not a little interest and the idea caught the attention of Richard Goold-Adams, the co-founder of the highly successful International Institute for Strategic Studies. A committee was formed under his leadership, which later became the 's.s. *Great Britain* Project'. The cost of salvage was largely solved when a great English patriot Mr. Jack Hayward donated £150,000 to the project. The San Francisco Museum generously withdrew from the scene and Dr. Corlett surveyed the ship in November 1968.

The full story of the ship and its return to Bristol has been told by Richard Goold-Adams in his fine book *The Return of the Great Britain*. Difficulties arose on all sides, not least among them the possibility that the crack in the *Great Britain's* starboard side would cause the ship to break her back. Salvage work started on March 25th, 1970 by an Anglo-German team, using the tug *Varius*, 724 tons, and the pontoon *Mulus III*. By April 14th, the *Great Britain* was aboard the pontoon and back in Port Stanley. The long voyage home began on April 24th and Bristolians had their first sight of the *Great Britain* since January 23rd, 1845 when she arrived at the mouth of the Avon on June 22nd, 1970. She had been away 125 years and 151 days.

Not everyone in Bristol greeted the returning ship with enthusiasm. The City Council was not entirely keen on this nostalgic venture. Its leaders were no different from past generations of Bristol shipowners who firmly believed that the only good ships were profitable ones, and they had a recurrent nightmare of a *Great Britain* abandoned on a reluctant Corporation, which would then have to stand all resultant costs. Nevertheless, the present author got a resolution through the controlling political group on July 4th, 1969, which accepted the ship into Bristol. The doubts were to remain for several years, but Bristol's acceptance of the

Great Britain dates from this resolution.

The *Varius* departed and King's *Sea Challenge* completed the tow into Avonmouth. The journey to Bristol had taken forty-nine days at an average speed of five knots. The *Great Britain* was removed from the pontoon, and, after a false start due to high winds the previous evening, she was towed up the river to the City Docks, in a four hour journey on the morning of Sunday July 5th, 1970.

The Plimsoll Swing Bridge, built 1961–64, to carry traffic over Cumberland Basin entrance locks. King's Sea Alert *and the* Beagle *are in the lock, together with sandsucker* Harry Brown.

The river bank was lined with cheering crowds as thousands of Bristolians turned out to watch and approve. Cars and tugs hooted a mutual chorus of welcome in the Avon Gorge. Confetti fell from Brunel's bridge onto Brunel's ship and then the harbour tugs eased her gently through the same entrance at Cumberland Basin that had given Brunel so much trouble all those years ago. Two weeks later, the *Great Britain* was moved into what proved to be her final resting place, the Wapping Dock in which she was built. As millions watched on television the old ship was edged slowly back into the dock. It was July 19th, 1970, exactly 127 years to the day after Prince Albert had helped Mrs. Miles to name the ship. H.R.H. Prince Philip, Duke of Edinburgh was on board for the occasion.

Today, ten years on, the *Great Britain*, with her bridge, funnel and two masts restored, is rapidly taking on the looks of a fully restored ship.

Bristol's second maritime boost in 1970 came after the General Election held in June of that year. The new Conservative administration under Edward Heath approved the City's scheme for a new deep water dock south of the River Avon at Portbury, between Portishead and the river mouth.

Years before, the ambitious Docks Committee, rightly judging that the size of ships would grow beyond the limits of its dock entrances, had quietly bought up the land needed for the new project. By the early 1950s, they were ready to proceed, and initial schemes for the Portbury site were drawn up. The first, published in 1960 was over-ambitious and turned down by the Minister of Transport. Although the committee did not realise it at the time, it was to take ten years of bitter controversy between Bristol and Whitehall before the necessary Government approval came about.

By the time the City submitted modified plans, Richard Marsh had become Transport Minister in Harold Wilson's Labour Government of the mid-1960s. He it was who once again turned down Bristol's proposal in a Government White Paper on transport in 1966. The Ministry argued that the P.B.A. had not calculated its forecasts on a sound economic basis and did not believe the new dock would be profitable. But all Bristol believed this to be only an excuse, and strongly suspected that the influence of the Welsh ports had much to do with the Government's decision. The arguments flew backwards and forwards between London,

Cardiff and Bristol in the years that followed but Bristol failed to change the Government's mind.

In 1969, in a letter to Eric Price, Editor of the *Western Daily Press,* the Bristol based daily newspaper, the Tory Leader of the Opposition, Edward Heath, said that a future ministry of his would give permission for West Dock but only on the understanding that the City of Bristol raise the cost of the project itself and there would be no government funding. When he entered No. 10, Ted Heath was as good as his word, and the Bristol West Dock Act received the Royal Assent on July 27th, 1971. Work commenced in April 1972 with a completion date set for 1975.

The new dock provides for ships up to about 75,000 tonnes carrying capacity. The water area is seventy acres and the planned depth of water forty-five feet. There are three quays each 2,000 feet long and the entrance lock measures 1,200 feet long by 140 feet wide, the largest in Britain.

As the new dock began to take shape, other forces were already gathering which would have dramatic and indeed disastrous impacts on the project's early years.

In 1973, as Bristol celebrated 600 years as a county (a status granted in a charter of Edward III) with a visit from Queen Elizabeth II, the 1972 Local Government Act came into force, reducing the City Council to a second tier authority and creating the County of Avon, a unit of local government that did the impossible by uniting Bristolians and Somerset men in common agreement that they detested the new arrangements.

Ashmead's tugs towing the new lockgates, Britain's largest, from their builder's yard at Chepstow to Royal Portbury Dock in 1976.

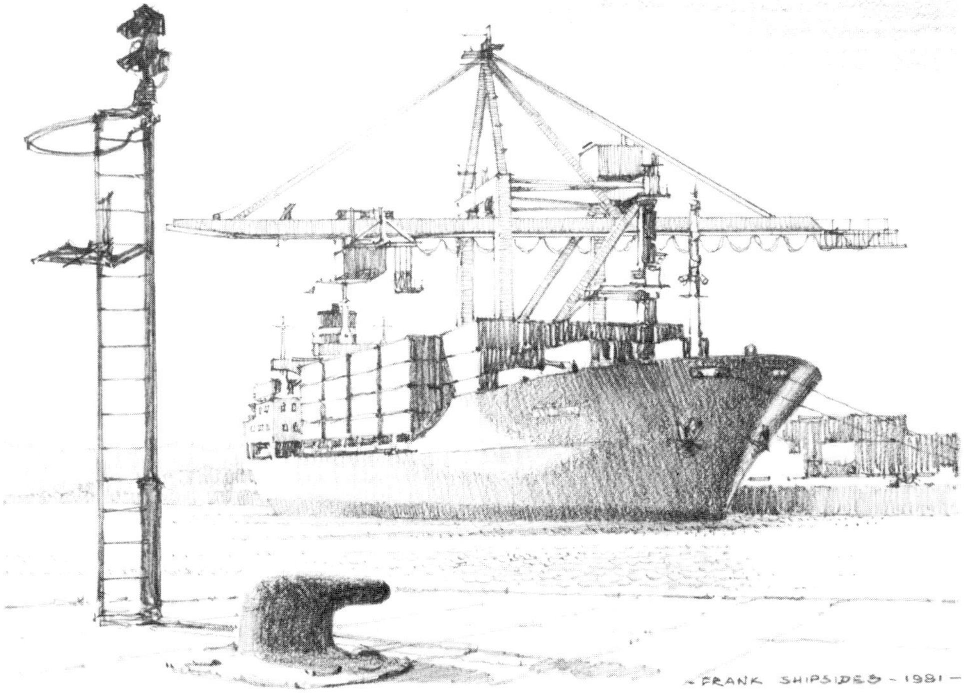

The twentieth century scene. A container ship docks at Royal Portbury Dock.

There were delays in the programme for West Dock and it was not until August 8th, 1977, that the tugs *Sea Merrimac, Sea Alert, Sea Volunteer* and *Sea Challenge* hauled the Royal Yacht *Britannia* into the Royal Portbury Dock, the name chosen by Queen Elizabeth, who was on board to perform the opening ceremony, just as her great-grandfather had opened the Royal Edward Dock in *Victoria and Albert* sixty-nine years before.

By this time, the grandiose scheme for new locks at the City Docks had proved to be beyond the means of the new City Council and the Bristol Corporation Act 1971 was abandoned on April 13th, 1976. Nevertheless, the transformation of the old City Docks into a residential, commercial and amenity area has made steady, if unspectacular, progress. The sand boats still come and go, and there are regular visits from naval vessels of NATO fleets. An industrial museum has been opened at Princes Wharf, to be followed by the R.N.L.I. National Museum. Hundreds of pleasure craft now crowd the quays where long ago the merchant venturers moored their vessels and each year the old quay walls vibrate to the screaming engines of power boats contesting the Embassy Grand Prix or echo to the laughter of thousands of slightly inebriated residents and visitors sampling the delights of the World Wine Fair, an annual event since 1978 and staged in old quayside transfer sheds along St. Augustines Reach.

At Avonmouth and Portbury, the world economic recession and record inflation of the late 1970s put paid to any hope Bristol had of immediate success at Royal Portbury, while trade at Avonmouth fell away. As the new decade of the 1980s began, the City found itself obliged to demand huge sums of money annually once again to support its port. The fight for commercial success was beginning all over again. Despite these difficult times, large ships began to call at the new dock. By July 1981, the largest so far was *Ortelius,* 52,444 g.r.t., which docked on February 2nd, 1979. As the Lord Mayor in 1977, the late Ted Wright, said in his speech of welcome to the Queen, Bristol had come to 'the end of the beginning'.

Bibliography and Sources

1. BOOKS (Specific to Bristol)
   The Annals of Bristol (4 vols.)—*Latimer, J.* (Bristol 1887–1908)
   The Merchant Venturers of Bristol—*McGrath, P.* (Bristol 1975)
   At the Port of Bristol (3 vols.)—*Neale, W. G.* (Bristol 1968–1976)
   A Short History of the Port of Bristol—*Wells, C.* (Bristol 1909)
   Bristol—As It Was and As It Is—*Stone, G. F.* (Bristol 1909)
   Shipshape and Bristol Fashion—*Hill, J. C. G.* (Liverpool 1956)
   Records of Bristol Ships—*Farr, G.* (Bristol 1950)
   Bristol—Gateway of Empire—*MacInnes, C.* (Bristol 1939)
   Bristol Privateers and Ships of War—*Powell, J. P.* (Bristol 1930)
   Bristol—*Hunt, W.* (London 1889)

2. BOOKS (General with reference to Bristol, the Port and Bristol Ships)
   West Country Passenger Steamers—*Farr, G.* (Prescot 1967)
   Bristol Channel Pleasure Steamers—*Wall, R.* (Newton Abbot 1973)
   The Return of the Great Britain—*Goold-Adams, R.* (London 1976)
   Wreck and Rescue in the Bristol Channel—*Farr, G.* (Truro 1966)
   The Sailing Pilots of the Bristol Channel—*Stuckey, P.* (Newton Abbot 1976)
   Lundy—*Langham, A. & L.* (Newton Abbot 1970)
   British Warships Names—*Manning & Walker* (London 1956)
   Merchant Ships—*Talbot-Booth, E. C.* (London 1943)
   Ocean Liners—*Wall, R.* (New York 1978)
   Major Seaports of the United Kingdom—*Bird, J.* (London 1963)

3. MONOGRAPHS
   Ship Building in the Port of Bristol—*Farr, G.* (London 1977)
   Bristol Branch of Historical Association (Port of Bristol Series)—*MacInnes, Farr et al.* (Bristol—Various)

4. NEWSPAPERS (On file Bristol Central Library)
Felix Farley's Journal
Clifton Chronicle
Times and Mirror
Western Daily Press
Bristol Evening World
Bristol Evening Post

5. RECORDS AND ARCHIVES
City Archives of the City of Bristol and Archives of the Port of Bristol
Library of the Port of Bristol
Bristol Dock Acts 1803–1972
Minutes of Council of City and County of Bristol to 1974
Minutes of Council of City of Bristol (1974–1981)
Minutes of the Port of Bristol Authority (Docks Committee)

Index of Ships

People, Places and Shipping Companies